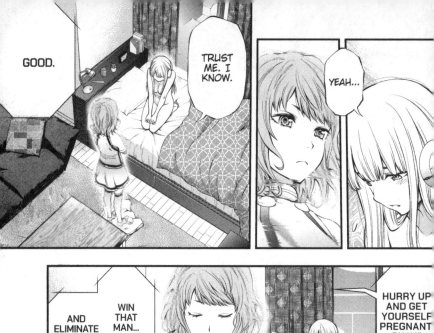

GOOD.

TRUST ME. I KNOW.

YEAH...

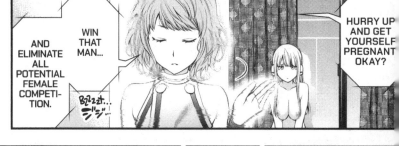

AND ELIMINATE ALL POTENTIAL FEMALE COMPETITION.

WIN THAT MAN...

Bzzzt...
ジジ..

HURRY UP AND GET YOURSELF PREGNANT OKAY?

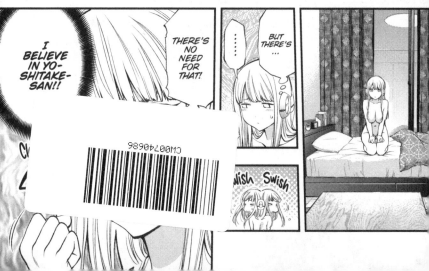

I BELIEVE IN YO-SHITAKE-SAN!!

THERE'S NO NEED FOR THAT!

....

BUT THERE'S...

Swish Swish

I BELIEVE IN HIM!!
ふー!
Spreead
くぱぁ
Huuuuff!
Huuuuff!
Huuuuff!
Noooooo!
PLEASE ...
HOLY SHIT! IT'S SUPER PINK!
ぱくぁー
Spreead
SHE'S SO WET...
PLEASE DON'T STARE AT IT...
omg...
THIS IS REALLY FUCKING SEXY!!

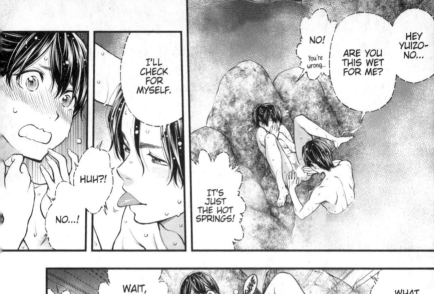

I'LL CHECK FOR MYSELF.

HUH?!

NO...!

IT'S JUST THE HOT SPRINGS!

NO! You're wrong...

ARE YOU THIS WET FOR ME?

HEY YUIZO-NO...

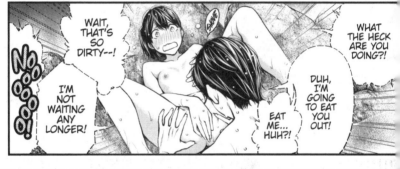

WAIT, THAT'S SO DIRTY--!

NOOOOOO!

I'M NOT WAITING ANY LONGER!

SAME

EAT ME... HUH?!

WHAT THE HECK ARE YOU DOING?!

DUH, I'M GOING TO EAT YOU OUT!

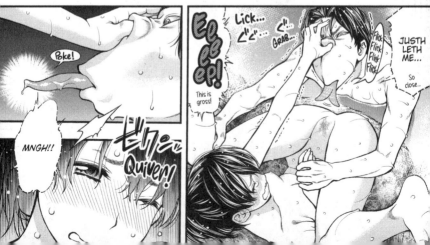

Poke!

MNGH!!

Quiver!

Lick... く゛く゛... く゛... GRAB...

This is gross!

JUSTH LETH ME...

Flick! Flick! Flick! Flick!

So close...

Schla-lick
ぬりゅん
Hngah!!
Quiiiiiiver!
Quiver!
STOP IT...
NO...
ANH!
Jolt!
HOLY SHIT...
ARE ALL PUSSIES SO SENSITIVE?!
THE LITTLEST LICK MADE HER PUSSY QUIVER...
Sqwiiish!
SO HOW ABOUT HER CLIT?!
KEEP QUIET...
Bwa ha ha ha!
Quit it, stupid!
HANH...
Jolt Jolt
EEEEP...!
HUFF...!
Quiver!

じゅ Hugh!
Sluuuuuuuuuurrp!
るるるるるるるるる
MNNNGH...
STOP SUCKING IT...
ビクッ Jolt
ビク… Quiver
Hnggggggh...
ビクッ Jolt
じゅる Shlurp
Shlp ぬる
WOW, SHE'S GETTING WETTER!
Shlup ぬちゅ
PAAANT ...!
HUUUFF ...!
IT'S SO SOFT AND SLIPPERY...
IT'S SUCKING ON MY TONGUE!!
にゅるる Shlick
ぷちゅ Shlk
ぷちゅる Supa-shlk
くりくりくりくりっ ThwpThwpThwpThwp
CLIT!
AH...!
SLIT!
Thwwwp-wha-whp くりりりりりり
ビクッ Quiver!
Hnnngh!!
Jolt! ビクッ
CLIT! SLIT!
UNGH...
ANH!
ビクッ Jolt!
べろべろべろべろ— Slurp Slurp Slurp Slurp
ANH!
Slurp Slurp Slurp Slurp べろべろべろべろ
ビクッ Jolt!
AAAANGH...
UMNF ...
CLIT!! SLIT!! CLIT!! SLIT!!
Jolt! Quiver! ビクビクッ

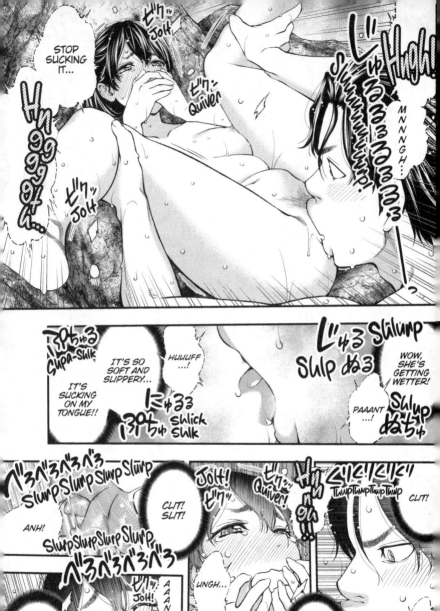

SLIT! SLIT! SLIT! SLIT! CLIT! CLIT! CLIT! CLIT! SLIT! CLIT! SLIT! CLIT! SLIT! CLIT! SLIT! CLIT!
Slurp Slurp Slurp Slurp Slurp Slurp Slurp Slurp Slurp Slurp
Wheeze ....!
SCLIT! SCLIT! SCLIT SCLLLLLLL-IIIIITTTTTT!!!
Jolt Jolt
Quiver!
Huga aaaaaaaaaaaaaaaaah! !!!...
Quiver
Slurp Slurp Slurp Slurp Slurp Slurp
Slurp Slurp Slurp Slurp Slurp Slurp
STOP IT... I'M GONNA CUM...!
Jolt!
Augh...
EWW, GROSS! THIS IS SO EMBARRASS-ING...! NOOO!
Aaaah...
Quiver
!

Screech
Screech
HUH...?
WHAT'S GOING ON?
WHO IS THIS?
Screech
SENPAI?
Screech
I'M SCARED...
NO, STOP! I'M SCARED!
MAKE IT STOP!!
Screech

Screech...
HE'S GOING TO KILL ME!!!

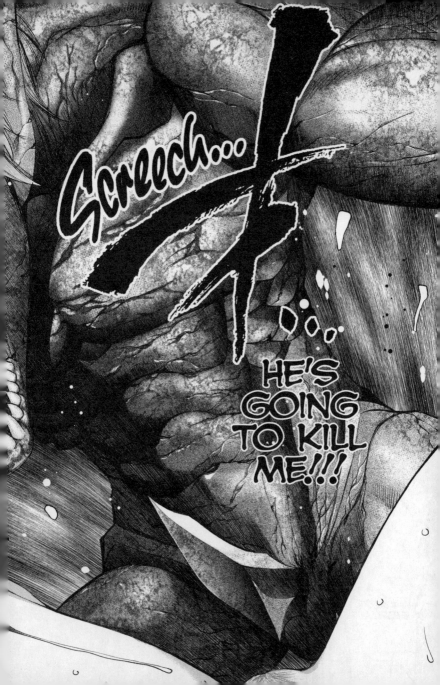

EEEP...!

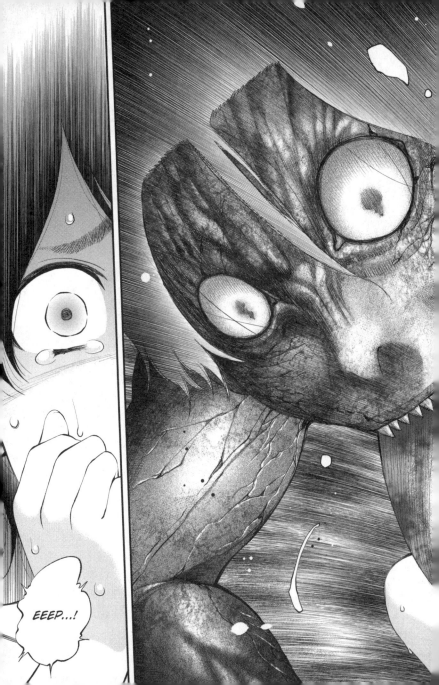

Nooo! No!
Ah!
Aoonh! Ah!
Aaaah...
Stomp
Stomp
Stomp
Stomp
WHA-BAM
Clatter
Stomp
SAAAAAAAAAAAAAAKUUUUUUUUUUUU
D HOTEL HAKKAI
GRAND HOTEL HAKKAI

RAAAAAA!!!...
Ken.
Thwaaack
UNNGH!!
YOU PIECE OF SHIT!!!
MNGH ... HNN-NGH ...!
I KNEW YOU WERE A HORNDOG DICKWAD...
BUT I NEVER THOUGHT YOU WERE A RAPIST!!
KIMI-JIMA-KUN!
HOW DARE YOU ASSAULT HARUKA!
THAT FUCKING HURTS, YOU BITCH! YOU KICK LIKE A MAN!
I'LL KILL YOU!!!
SHOULD WE INVOLVE THE POLICE?
NO, IT'LL MAKE IT WORSE.
YOU'LL PAY FOR THIS!
WAIT, GOD-DAMN IT!
Listen to me!
YOU THINK THIS COULD BE WORSE?!
BUT SIR...

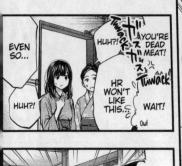

EVEN SO...

HUH?!

HUH?!

YOU'RE DEAD MEAT!

HR WON'T LIKE THIS.

WAIT!

Ow!

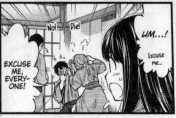

No! Die!

EXCUSE ME, EVERY- ONE!

UM...!

Excuse me...

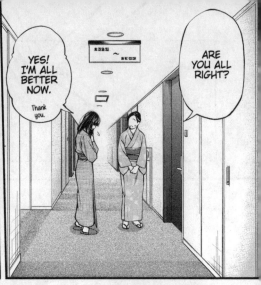

YES! I'M ALL BETTER NOW.

Thank you.

ARE YOU ALL RIGHT?

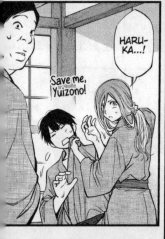

HARU- KA...!

Save me, Yuizono!

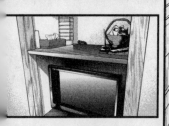

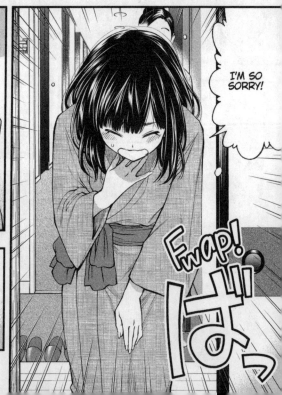

I'M SO SORRY!

Fwap!

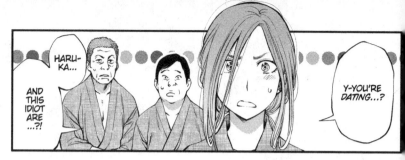

HARU-KA... AND THIS IDIOT ARE...?!

Y-YOU'RE DATING...?

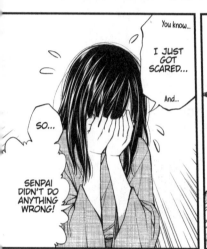

You know... I JUST GOT SCARED... And...

SO...

SENPAI DIDN'T DO ANYTHING WRONG!

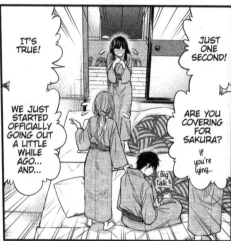

IT'S TRUE!

WE JUST STARTED OFFICIALLY GOING OUT A LITTLE WHILE AGO... AND...

JUST ONE SECOND!

ARE YOU COVERING FOR SAKURA? If you're lying...

Big talk!

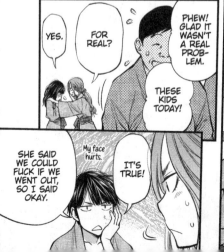

YES.

FOR REAL?

PHEW! GLAD IT WASN'T A REAL PROBLEM.

THESE KIDS TODAY!

SHE SAID WE COULD FUCK IF WE WENT OUT, SO I SAID OKAY.

My face hurts.

IT'S TRUE!

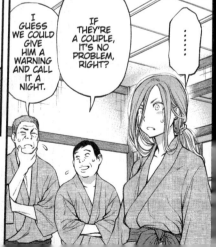

I GUESS WE COULD GIVE HIM A WARNING AND CALL IT A NIGHT.

IF THEY'RE A COUPLE, IT'S NO PROBLEM, RIGHT?

......

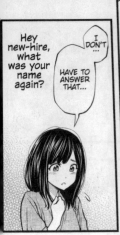

Hey new-hire, what was your name again?

I DON'T... HAVE TO ANSWER THAT...

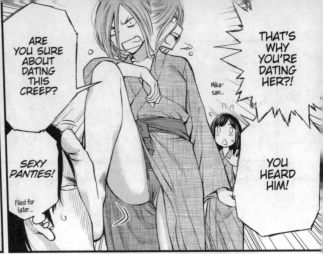

ARE YOU SURE ABOUT DATING THIS CREEP?

SEXY PANTIES!

Filed for later...

THAT'S WHY YOU'RE DATING HER?!

Mika-san...

YOU HEARD HIM!

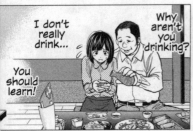

I don't really drink...

Why aren't you drinking?

You should learn!

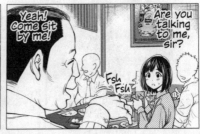

Yeah! Come sit by me!

Fsh Fsh

Are you talking to me, sir?

Bottle: Daiginjo Tsuyusato Tsuruyama

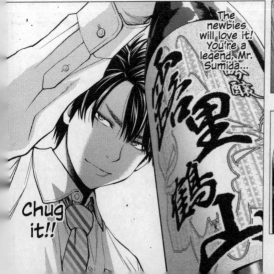

The newbies will love it! You're a legend, Mr. Sumida...

chug it!!

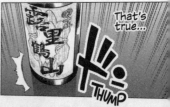

That's true...

THUMP

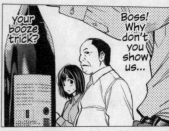

your booze trick?

Boss! Why don't you show us...

18

Phuhh...
Time to go home!

Cheer ドン･チャン Chatter やんや
Chatter ドン･チャン
Cheer やんや

Sea Go home?!

Just flatter annoying people and help them get drunk!

That's how it's done!

C'mon. New hires don't have to stay.

EVER SINCE I STARTED...

YOSHITAKE, HE...

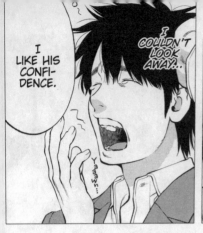

I LIKE HIS CONFIDENCE.

I COULDN'T LOOK AWAY...

Yaaah...

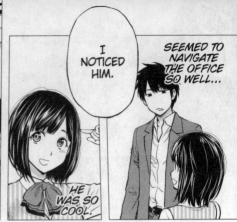

I NOTICED HIM.

SEEMED TO NAVIGATE THE OFFICE SO WELL...

HE WAS SO COOL.

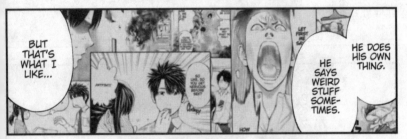

BUT THAT'S WHAT I LIKE...

HE SAYS WEIRD STUFF SOMETIMES.

HE DOES HIS OWN THING.

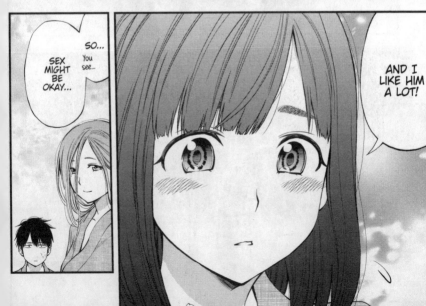

SO... You see...

SEX MIGHT BE OKAY...

AND I LIKE HIM A LOT!

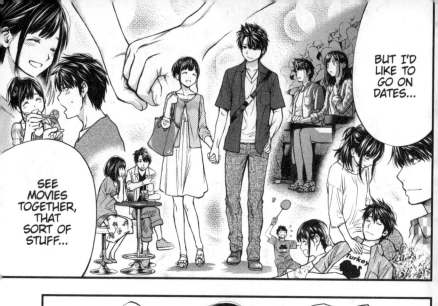

BUT I'D LIKE TO GO ON DATES...

SEE MOVIES TOGETHER, THAT SORT OF STUFF...

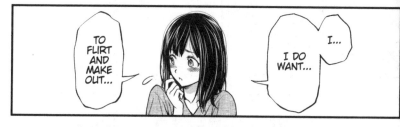

TO FLIRT AND MAKE OUT...

I DO WANT...

I...

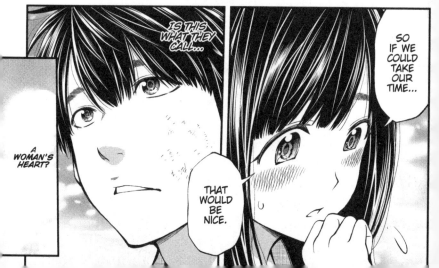

IS THIS WHAT THEY CALL...

A WOMAN'S HEART?

SO IF WE COULD TAKE OUR TIME...

THAT WOULD BE NICE.

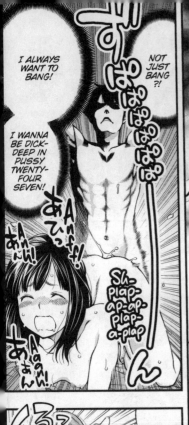

I ALWAYS WANT TO BANG!

NOT JUST BANG?!

I WANNA BE DICK-DEEP IN PUSSY TWENTY-FOUR SEVEN!

Sh-plap-ap-ap-plap-a-plap

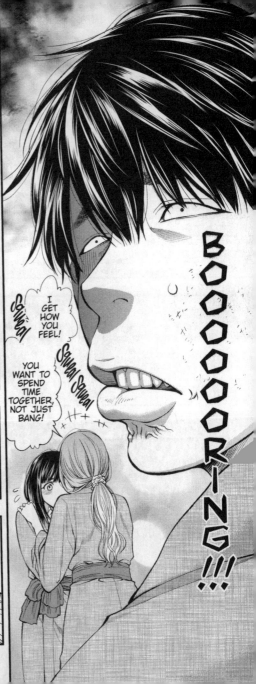

BOOOOORING!!!

I GET HOW YOU FEEL!

YOU WANT TO SPEND TIME TOGETHER, NOT JUST BANG!

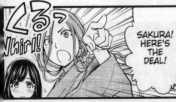

SAKURA! HERE'S THE DEAL!

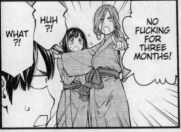

WHAT?!

HUH?!

NO FUCKING FOR THREE MONTHS!

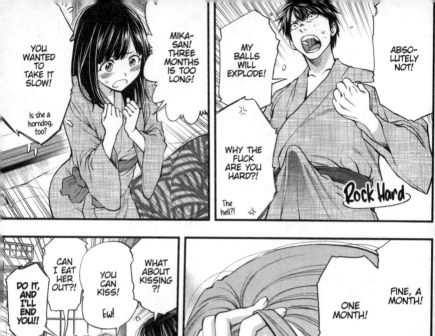

YOU WANTED TO TAKE IT SLOW!

Is she a horndog, too?

MIKA-SAN! THREE MONTHS IS TOO LONG!

MY BALLS WILL EXPLODE!

ABSO-LUTELY NOT!

WHY THE FUCK ARE YOU HARD?!

The hell?!

Rock Hard

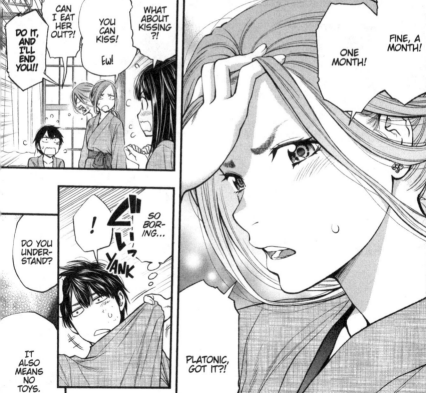

CAN I EAT HER OUT?!

DO IT, AND I'LL END YOU!!

YOU CAN KISS!

EW!

WHAT ABOUT KISSING?!

FINE, A MONTH!

ONE MONTH!

SO BOR-ING...

!

YANK

DO YOU UNDER-STAND?

IT ALSO MEANS NO TOYS.

PLATONIC, GOT IT?!

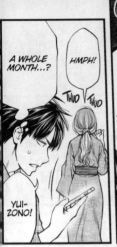

A WHOLE MONTH...?

HMPH!

THUD THUD

YUI-ZONO!

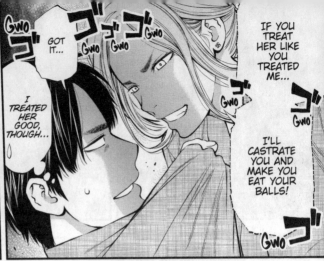

GWO ゴ ゴ GWO GWO GWO

GOT IT...

I TREATED HER GOOD, THOUGH...

IF YOU TREAT HER LIKE YOU TREATED ME...

GWO ゴ

GWO ゴ

I'LL CASTRATE YOU AND MAKE YOU EAT YOUR BALLS!

GWO ゴ

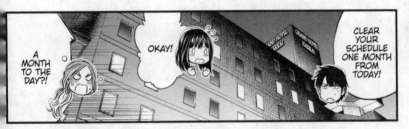

A MONTH TO THE DAY?!

OKAY!

CLEAR YOUR SCHEDULE ONE MONTH FROM TODAY!

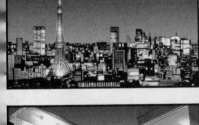

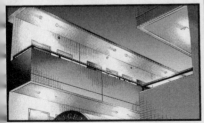

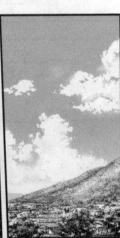

24

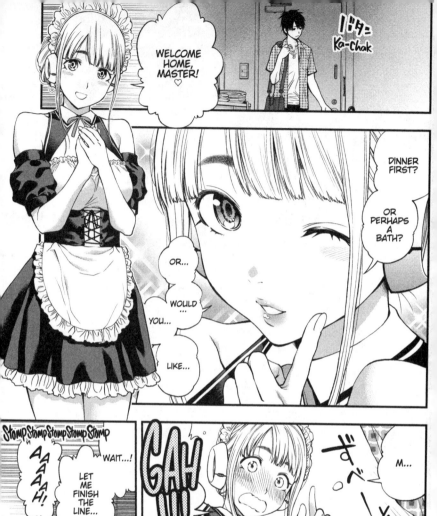

WELCOME HOME, MASTER! ♡

ヒ゛ッタ゜ニ Ka-chak

DINNER FIRST?

OR PERHAPS A BATH?

OR...

WOULD...

YOU...

LIKE...

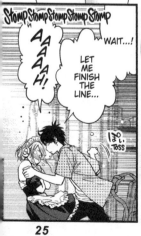

STOMP STOMP STOMP STOMP STOMP

AAAAH!

WAIT...!

LET ME FINISH THE LINE...

ぽい TOSS

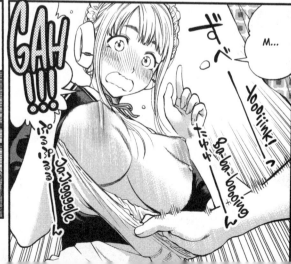

GAH!!!

M...

ずべ

Yooiiink!

Ba-ba-booing↑

Ba-Joggle

ぶるぶるぶる

25

YOU MASTURBATED WHILE I WAS GONE, RIGHT?
ドキー!
Ba-Bump
もんにゅ
squish
WHAAAAT?!
もんにゅ
squish
NO WAY!
LIAR! HOW MANY TIMES?!
NOT AT ALL!
REEEALLY? YOU SURE?
Thp Thp Thp Thp Thp Thp
NO...!
I DIDN'T DO IT...
NN...!
Sqsh
Sqsh
Sqsh
JUST LIKE THIS...!
ゴロッ
Roll
NO...!

ARE YOU SUUURE?!
SCHLIIIIIIIIIICCCKKK!
ぬりゅぬりゅぬりゅ
Shlick Shlick Shlick
Anh!
No!
TAKE THIS! AND THIS! AND THIS! AND THIS!!
Squilch Squilch
Squilch Squilch
HOW DO YOU LIKE THIS, HUH? TELL ME THE TRUTH, BITCH!!
Squilch Squilch Squilch
Aaanh! Aaaaaaaaannngh...
Squilch Squilch Squilch
PLEASE DON'T BE SO ROUGH WITH ME!
Squelch Squelch
Schlwip Schlwip
Anh! Ah...!
Thwip

Schla-lick!
Splup
Quiiiiiver!
Aaaanh...!

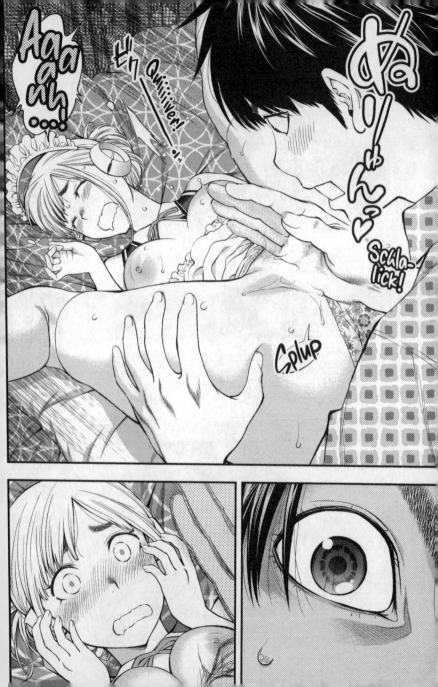

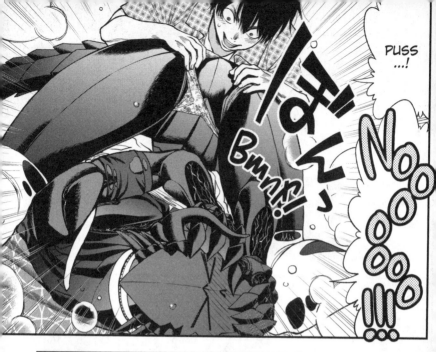

PUSS ...!

NOOOOOOO!!!!

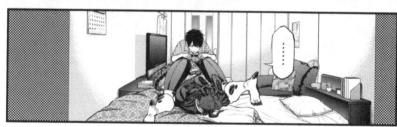

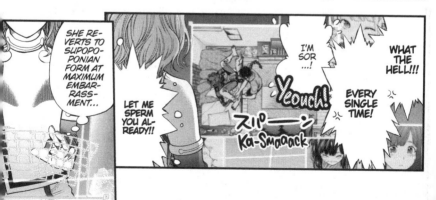

SHE REVERTS TO SUPOPOPONIAN FORM AT MAXIMUM EMBARRASSMENT...

LET ME SPERM YOU ALREADY!!

I'M SOR...!

Yeouch!
スパーン
Ka-Smaaack

WHAT THE HELL!!!

EVERY SINGLE TIME!

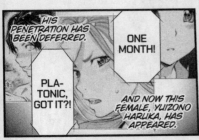

HIS PENETRATION HAS BEEN DEFERRED.

ONE MONTH!

PLA-TONIC, GOT IT?!

AND NOW THIS FEMALE, YUIIZONO HARUKA, HAS APPEARED.

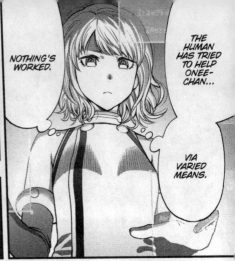

NOTHING'S WORKED.

THE HUMAN HAS TRIED TO HELP ONEE-CHAN...

VIA VARIED MEANS.

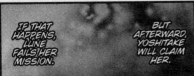

IF THAT HAPPENS, LUNE FAILS HER MISSION.

BUT, AFTERWARD, YOSHITAKE WILL CLAIM HER.

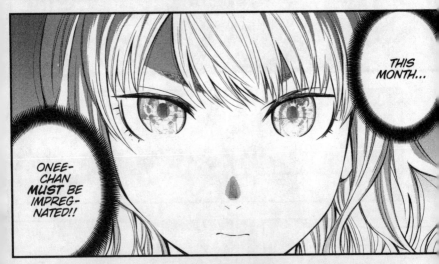

THIS MONTH...

ONEE-CHAN MUST BE IMPREGNATED!!

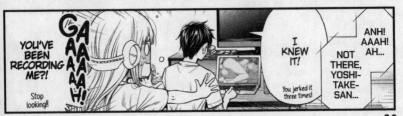

YOU'VE BEEN RECORDING ME?!

Stop looking!!

GAAAAAH!

I KNEW IT!

You jerked it three times!

NOT THERE, YOSHI-TAKE-SAN...

ANH! AAAH! AH...

30

Stopping Point
07
First Date at an Amusement Park!

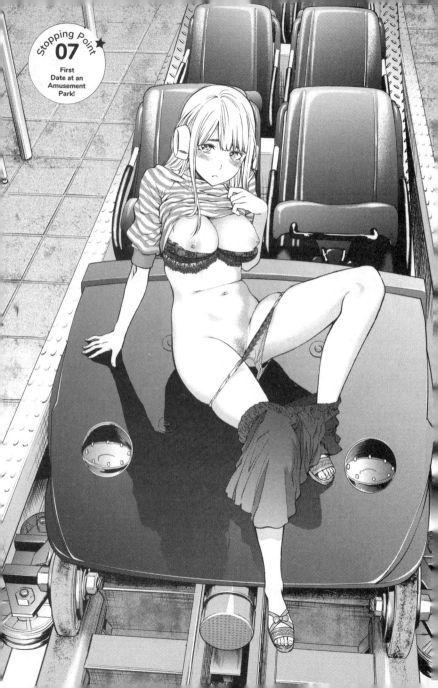

オメーションセンター
INFOMATION CENTER
MORN-IN'...
ARGH! THERE YOU ARE!
Ten minutes late!
MITSUKOSH
IT'S EIGHT IN THE MORNING ON A SATURDAY!
YOU COULD HAVE TEXTED...
YEAH, YEAH. MY BAD.
Yaoawn...
SO?
WHERE DID YOU WANT TO GO?
JEEZ!
I TOLD YOU YESTER-DAY!
WHAT A SLOB...
Yawning...?
TODAY, SAKURA-SENPAI AND I...

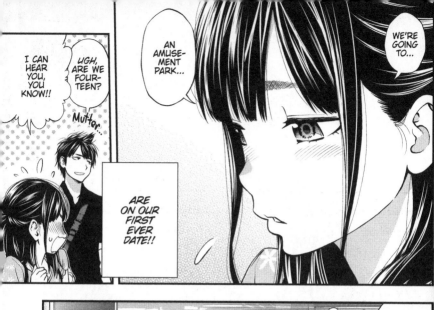

WE'RE GOING TO...

AN AMUSE-MENT PARK...

UGH, ARE WE FOUR-TEEN?

I CAN HEAR YOU, YOU KNOW!!

Mutter...

ARE ON OUR FIRST EVER DATE!!

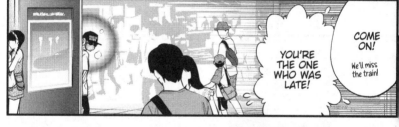

COME ON!

We'll miss the train!

YOU'RE THE ONE WHO WAS LATE!

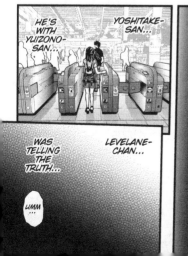

HE'S WITH YUIIZONO-SAN...

YOSHITAKE-SAN...

WAS TELLING THE TRUTH...

LEVELANE-CHAN...

UMM...

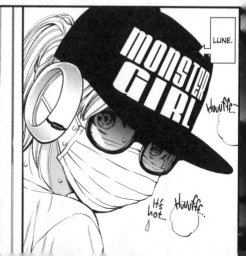

LUNE.

MONSTER GIRL

Huuuffl...

It's hot...

Huuuffl...

COULD YOU...
SAY THAT AGAIN ...?
YOU HEARD ME!
AS I PREDICT-ED...
Bzz... Bzz...
YOUR SPERM DONOR IS DATING!
CRUUUUUUSHED
IT CAN'T BE...
Plip Plip Plip
THIS IS YOUR FAULT!
WHO IS IT ...?
YUIZONO HARUKA! THE FEMALE FROM HIS OFFICE!
WHY ARE YOU CRY-ING?!
YOUR MISSION IS TO GET HIS SPERM!
THIS ISN'T ABOUT FEELINGS!

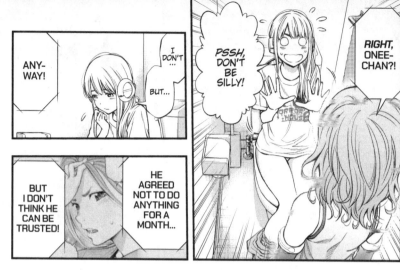

ANY-WAY!

I DON'T...

BUT...

PSSH, DON'T BE SILLY!

RIGHT, ONEE-CHAN?!

BUT I DON'T THINK HE CAN BE TRUSTED!

HE AGREED NOT TO DO ANYTHING FOR A MONTH...

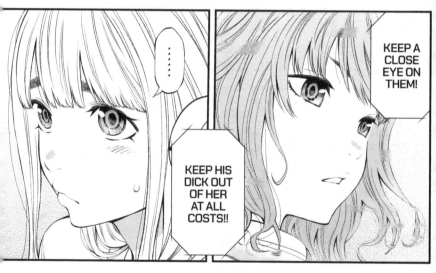

......

KEEP A CLOSE EYE ON THEM!

KEEP HIS DICK OUT OF HER AT ALL COSTS!!

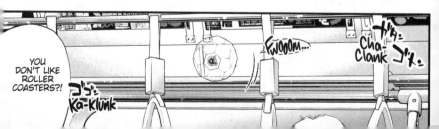

YOU DON'T LIKE ROLLER COASTERS?!

ゴゴ、 Ka-Klunk

Fwooom...

ガガ、 Cha-Clank ゴゴ、

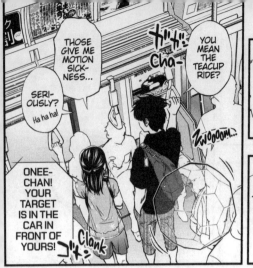

THOSE GIVE ME MOTION SICKNESS...

SERIOUSLY? Ha ha ha!

YOU MEAN THE TEACUP RIDE?

Zwooom...

ONEE-CHAN! YOUR TARGET IS IN THE CAR IN FRONT OF YOURS!

Clank

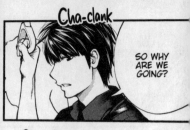

Cha-clank

SO WHY ARE WE GOING?

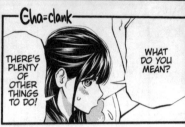

Cha-clank

THERE'S PLENTY OF OTHER THINGS TO DO!

WHAT DO YOU MEAN?

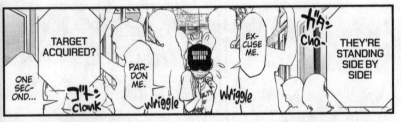

TARGET ACQUIRED?

ONE SECOND...

Clank

PARDON ME.

Wriggle

EXCUSE ME.

Wriggle

THEY'RE STANDING SIDE BY SIDE!

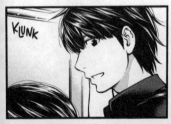

KLUNK

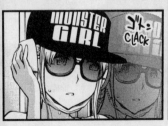

Clack

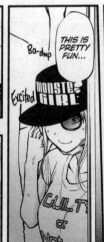

Ba-dmp

THIS IS PRETTY FUN...

Excited

MONSTER GIRL

CULT or

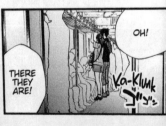

THERE THEY ARE!

OH!

Ka-Klunk

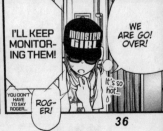

I'LL KEEP MONITORING THEM!

WE ARE GO! OVER!

It's so hot!

YOU DON'T HAVE TO SAY ROGER...

ROG-ER!

36

Didn't I tell you I'd be the one to pop your alien cherry?!
I'm going to sperm you until you're preg-nant!!
I swear it!!
YOSHITAKE-SAN...
You will bear my child!
ゴ RMMMbbbIII
ワー Rooooaaaar
キャー Squeeeaaal
ワー Rooaaaaar
ぱあぁ Shaaa-
Shing! ああっ

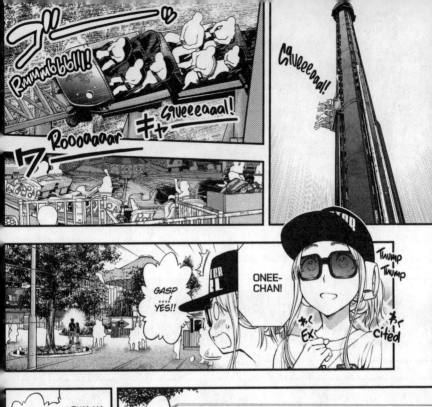

GASP....! YES!!

ONEE-CHAN!

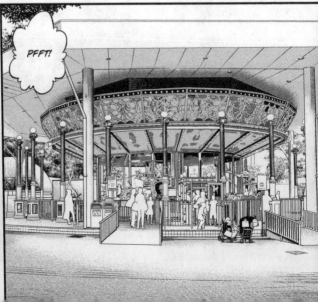

PFFT!

BWA HA HA HA! I CAN'T BELIEVE IT.

IT'S A KIDDIE RIDE!

AND WHAT'S WRONG WITH THAT?!

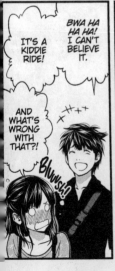

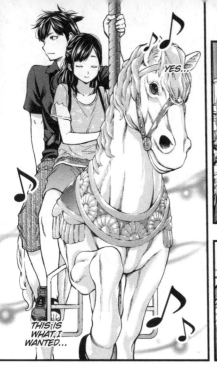

YES...

THIS IS WHAT I WANTED...

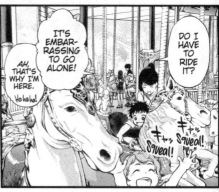

IT'S EMBARRASSING TO GO ALONE!

AH, THAT'S WHY I'M HERE.

Ha ha ha!

DO I HAVE TO RIDE IT?

キャッ SQUEAL!

キャッ SQUEAL!

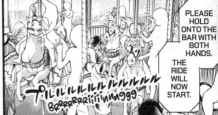

PLEASE HOLD ONTO THE BAR WITH BOTH HANDS.

THE RIDE WILL NOW START.

ルルルルルルルルルルルルル BRRRRRIIIINNNGGG

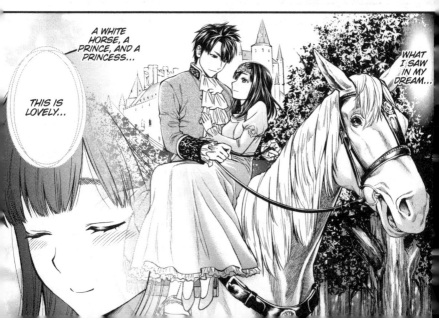

A WHITE HORSE, A PRINCE, AND A PRINCESS...

THIS IS LOVELY...

WHAT I SAW IN MY DREAM...

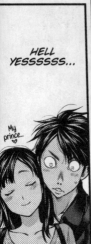

HELL YESSSSSS...

My prince... ♥

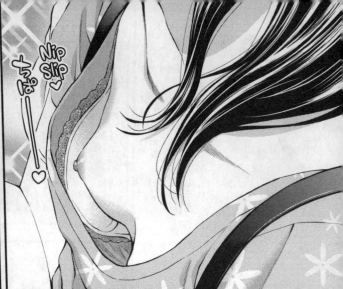

どきっ Nip Slip ♥

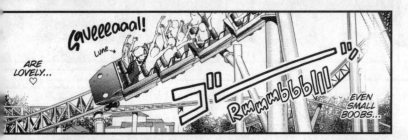

Gueeeaaal!

Lune →

Rmmmbbbll

ゴ"

ARE LOVELY... ♥

EVEN SMALL BOOBS...

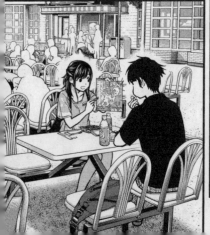

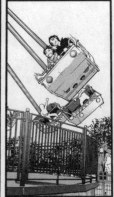

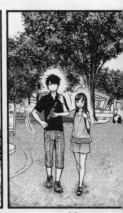

40

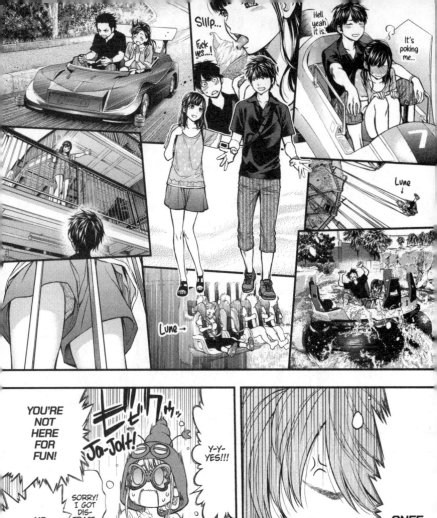

SIIIp...

Fuck yes...!

Hell yeah it is!

It's poking me...

Lune→

Lune→

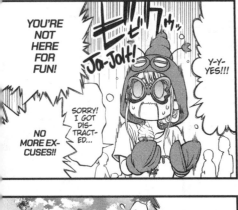

YOU'RE NOT HERE FOR FUN!

Ja-Jolt!

Y-Y-YES!!!

SORRY! I GOT DISTRACTED...

NO MORE EXCUSES!!

ONEE-CHAN?!!!

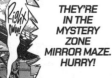

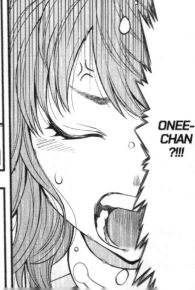

THEY'RE IN THE MYSTERY ZONE MIRROR MAZE. HURRY!

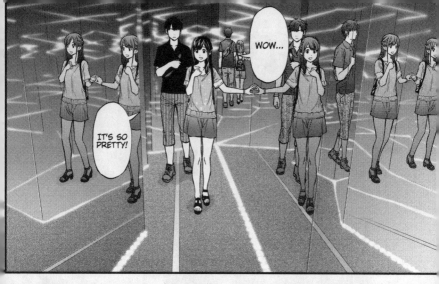

WOW...

IT'S SO PRETTY!

COME ON, LET'S GO!

THERE'S A HIDDEN DOOR HERE!

WHOA!

Cleak...

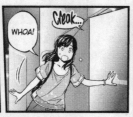

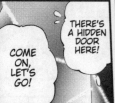

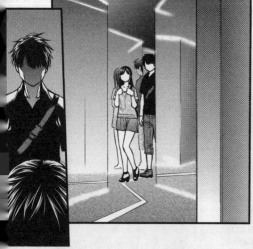

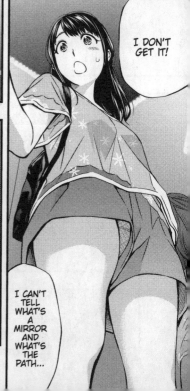

I DON'T GET IT!

I CAN'T TELL WHAT'S A MIRROR AND WHAT'S THE PATH...

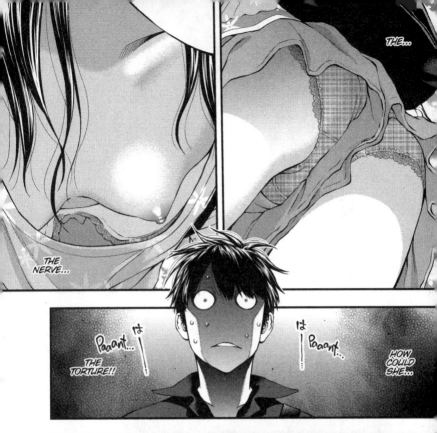

THE...

THE
NERVE...

Paaant... は

Paaant... は

THE
TORTURE!!

HOW
COULD
SHE...

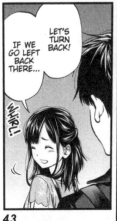

LET'S
TURN
BACK!

IF WE
GO LEFT
BACK
THERE...

WHIRL!

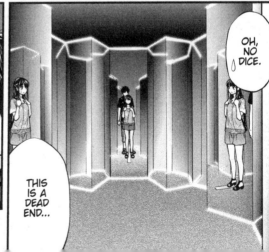

OH,
NO
DICE.

THIS
IS A
DEAD
END...

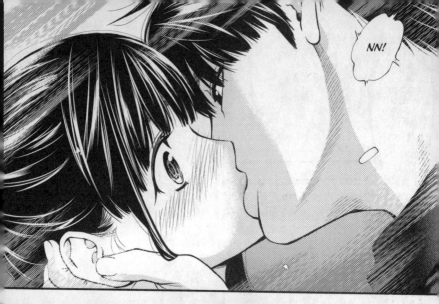

NN!

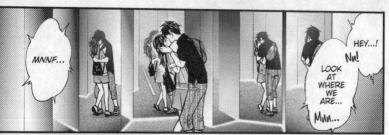

MNNF...

HEY...!

NN!

LOOK AT WHERE WE ARE...

MNN...

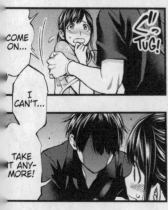

COME ON...

TUG!

I CAN'T...

TAKE IT ANY-MORE!

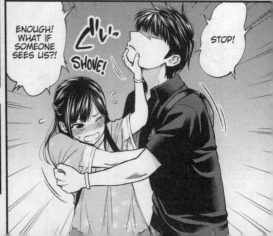

ENOUGH! WHAT IF SOMEONE SEES US?!

SHOVE!

STOP!

ALL YOU'VE DONE TODAY IS FLASH YOUR NIPPLES AND ASS!!
GRAAAAAAAA
がぁああああ
YOU'VE INVOKED THE WRATH OF THE DICK GOD!
AAAAH!
NIP-PLES...
ぼっ
Fwap!
YOU COULD SEE THEM?!
DON'T YOU GET IT?!
I'M ALWAYS LOOK-ING!!
I'M HORNY ALL THE TIME!!
Screeeeeeeeeeech!
Strategically Placed Ray of Light
I CAN'T CUM ENOUGH!!
SOCIETY FORCES ME TO HOLD BACK...
SO WHEN YOU SHOW OFF YOUR SEXY BODY...

FEEL THE WRATH OF THE DICK GOD!!!
ずぶ
NOOOOOO!!!......
YOOOOOINK!
ぷりーん
Jiggle
Schlick♥
WHAT IF SOMEONE COMES...
JOLT
OH, YOU'LL BE COMING!
Quiver!
Nn...! Ah!
DO IT FAST AND NO ONE WILL SEE.
No one's in this lame maze.
Schwp Schwp Schwp Schwp Schwp
Jolt!
Nn...!
WE'RE SUPPOSED TO WAIT A MONTH!
Mika-san said...
Ah...
Anh!
Quiver!
ぬちぬちぬち
Shlp Shlp Shlp
SO WHAT? THAT WHOLE THING WAS WEIRD.
Hunuff!
Shlp Shlp Shlp Shlp
ぬちぬちぬち
Shlp shlp ぬちぬちぬち
LOOK...
Pant
くいっ
TUG
TAKE A GOOD LOOK.
Unh

WITH THAT NAUGHTY FACE...
Nn...
No!
Pant...
THAT'S IT!
OH NO...
Quiver
Jolt!
An...
Rub
Rub
Ah...!
THIS IS SO EMBARRASSING...
Jolt!
Quiver!
Thwp
Thwp Thwp
THIS IS WRONG...
Pant...!
No...
Anh...!
EMBARRASSING...
Thwp
Thwp
Jolt!
Slup
BUT IT FEELS GOOD...
Aaanh...!
Slup
Slup
Tremble
Tremble
Slup
Aaanh!
I CAN'T FIGHT BACK...
Tremble
Slup
Slup
Quiver!
OH NO...
Jolt
Aaaaaaaaaaanh!
Jolt!

あ
Ah!
あ
Ah!
ゾクーーンッ
Quiiiiiiiivvvver!
I'M GONNA CUUUUUM ...!!!
あ
Ah!

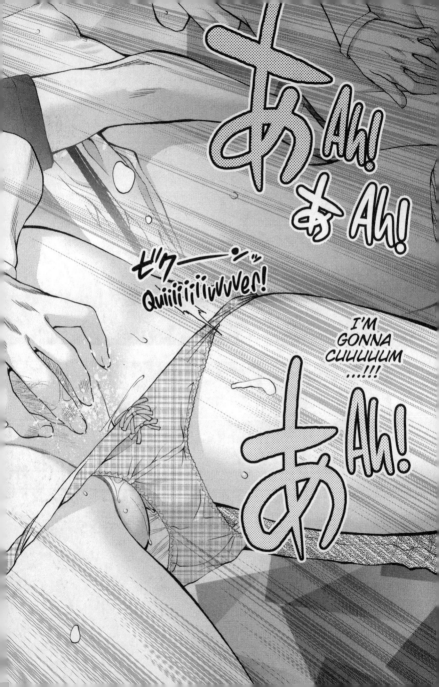

あ Ah!
ゾクッ Jolt!
Ah! あ
ゾクンッ Quiver!
Ah! あ
Ah! あ

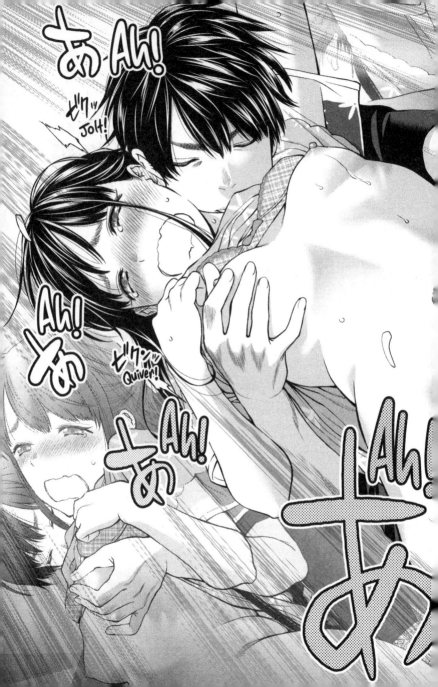

Hngah...
Shlp Shlp Shlp Shlp Shlp Shlp Shlp Shlp
IS HE GON-NA...
Slup Slup Slup Slup Slup Slup Slup
Nn...!
OUR FIRST TIME...
IN A PLACE LIKE THIS?!
Huff...
Ah!
Quiver!
Shlurp Shlurp Shlurp Shlurp Shlurp Shlurp Shlurp Shlurp
Jolt!
Aaah...
Quiver!
LIKE I SAID, GO RIGHT!
WHICH RIGHT?
AT THE FIVE-WAY JUNC-TION!!
WHICH IS RIGHT?
GO RIGHT, ONEE-CHAN!
I DON'T KNOW WHERE I AM ANY-MORE...
YOU'RE SO STU-PID!
EY!
AT THAT MOMENT, LUNE...

Stopping Point
08
No Hotels!!

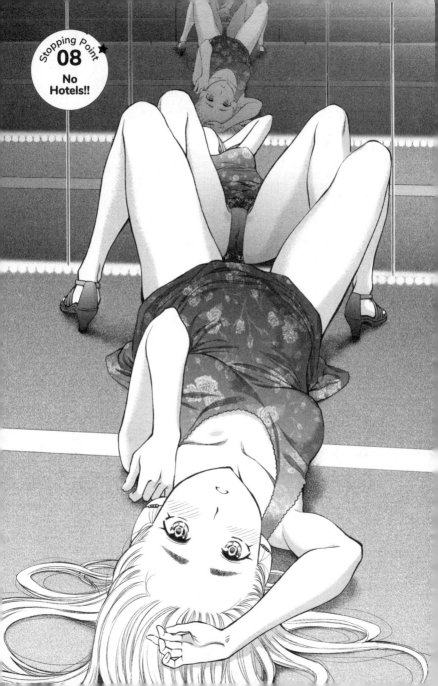

I CAN'T BELIEVE HE'S PUTTING IT INSIDE...
PANT...
NN...
Shiver!
Quiver!
HUFF...
Shwp Shwp
ShwpShwpShwp
IT'S HAPPEN-ING...
Umm...
HE'S GOING TO FUCK HER HERE?!
ONEECHAN! GO RIGHT! THEN LEFT!
HUH?!
WHAT?!
AHEAD FOUR POINT FIVE METERS. THERE'LL BE A HIDDEN DOOR ON YOUR LEFT. GO THROUGH, THEN TAKE A RIGHT AT THE FIRST INTERSECTION!
THEN YOU GO STRAIGHT AHEAD! HURRY!
HUUUUH?!
YOU...
GO! NOW!!
YOU'RE CONFUS-ING ME...

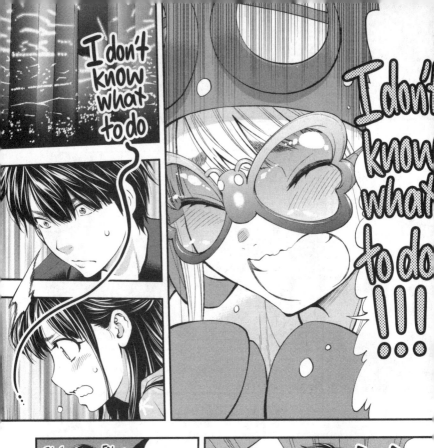

I don't know what to do

I don't know what to do!!!!!!

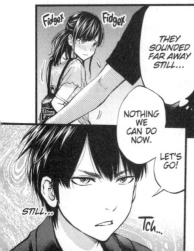

Fidget Fidget

THEY SOUNDED FAR AWAY STILL...

NOTHING WE CAN DO NOW.

LET'S GO!

STILL...

Tch...

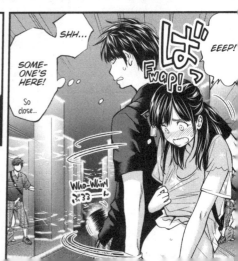

SHH...

SOME-ONE'S HERE!

So close...

ばっ
Fwap!

EEEP!

Who-Whirl
じゃ"ゎゎーム

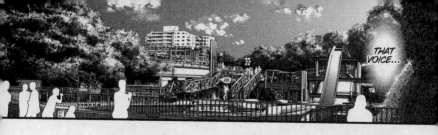

THAT VOICE...

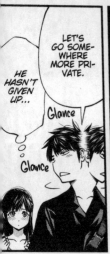

LET'S GO SOMEWHERE MORE PRIVATE.

HE HASN'T GIVEN UP...

Glance

Glance

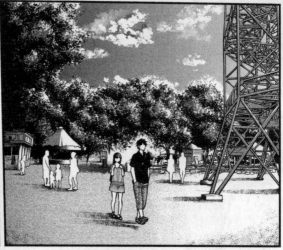

WHAT'S WRONG?

?

HEY, SAKURA-SENPAI...?

. . . . . .

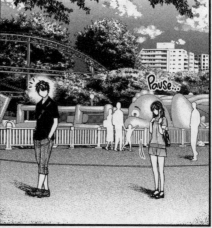

Pause...

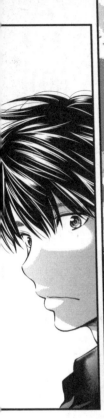
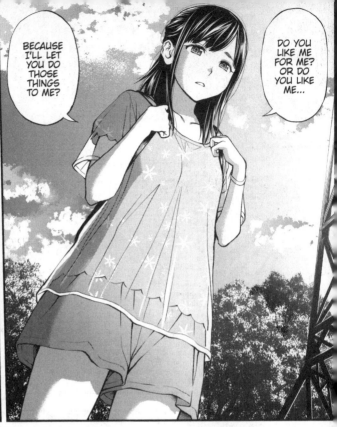

BECAUSE I'LL LET YOU DO THOSE THINGS TO ME?

DO YOU LIKE ME FOR ME? OR DO YOU LIKE ME...

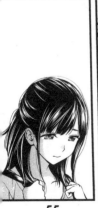
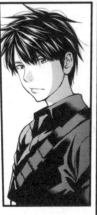
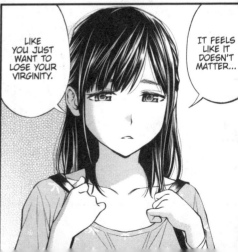

LIKE YOU JUST WANT TO LOSE YOUR VIRGINITY.

IT FEELS LIKE IT DOESN'T MATTER...

You fool!!!
ビクゥッ
JOOOLT!
HUNGH?!
IF IT DIDN'T MATTER, I'D HIRE A SEX WORKER!
HEY NOW...!
I COULD LOSE MY VIRGINITY WHENEVER I WANT!!
BUT I CHOOSE NOT TO!
IT'S NOT MY STYLE!!
BOOM!
IT DOESN'T SEEM FUN TO ME!!
YOU'RE YELL-ING...
Did he just yell "virginity"?
What's going on?
I...
WANT TO DO IT WITH A WOMAN OF MY CHOICE!!

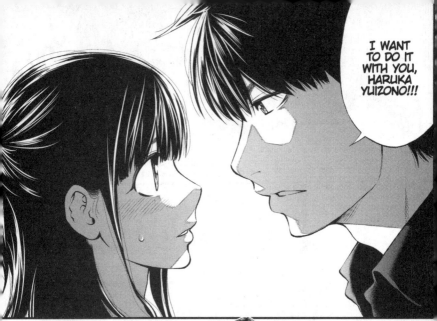

I WANT TO DO IT WITH YOU, HARUKA YUIZONO!!!

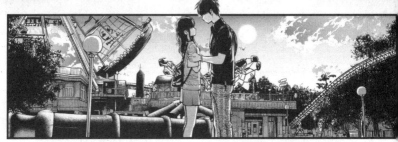

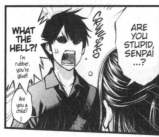

WHAT THE HELL?!

CRUSHED

I'm rubber, you're glue!!

Are you a child?

ARE YOU STUPID, SENPAI...?

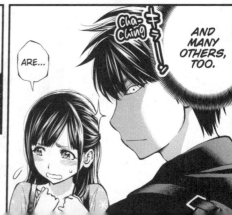

ARE...

Cha-Ching

AND MANY OTHERS, TOO.

FINE.

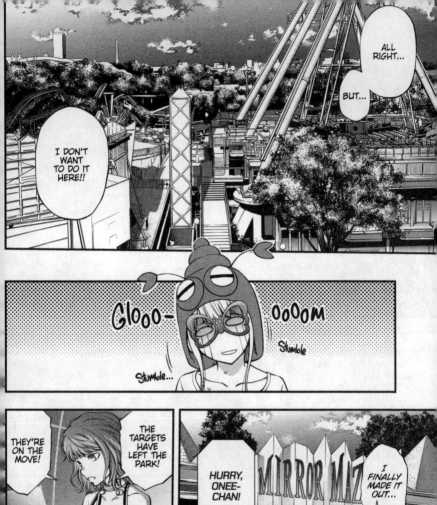

ALL RIGHT...

BUT...

I DON'T WANT TO DO IT HERE!!

Gloo-—oooom

Stumble...

Stumble

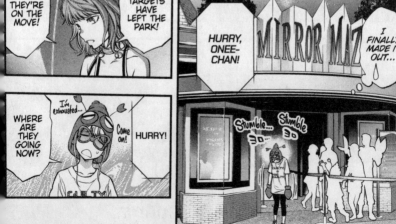

THEY'RE ON THE MOVE!

THE TARGETS HAVE LEFT THE PARK!

WHERE ARE THEY GOING NOW?

I'm exhausted...

Come on!

HURRY!

HURRY, ONEE-CHAN!

MIRROR MAZ

I FINALLY MADE IT OUT...

Stumble...

Stumble

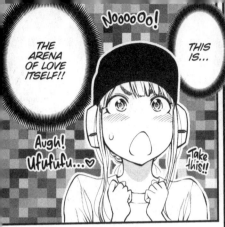

NoooOoOo!

THE ARENA OF LOVE ITSELF!!

THIS IS...

Augh! Ufufufu...♡

Take this!!

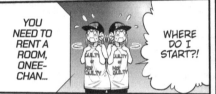

YOU NEED TO RENT A ROOM, ONEE-CHAN...

WHERE DO I START?!

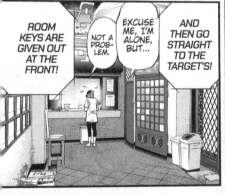

ROOM KEYS ARE GIVEN OUT AT THE FRONT!

NOT A PROB-LEM.

EXCUSE ME, I'M ALONE, BUT...

AND THEN GO STRAIGHT TO THE TARGET'S!

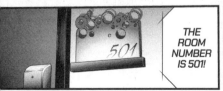

THE ROOM NUMBER IS 501!

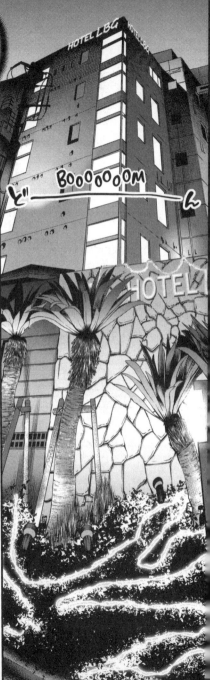

BOooOoOOM

HOTEL

Fsss-
SSS-SSh-hhh
PANT...
PANT...
THIS IS THE RUMORED VISIBLE SHOWER...
Long live one-way mirrors!!
Pant...!
YUI-ZONO'S PUSSY, IN REAL LIFE!!
Pant...!
I CAN'T FUCKING GET ENOUGH!!
THE FEMALE IS IN THE SHOWER. NOW'S YOUR CHANCE!
THE DOOR'S UN-LOCKED!
OKAY...
Ka-Chak Creak...
!
Ka-Chak
HUH?

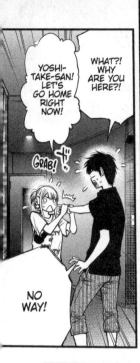

YOSHI-TAKE-SAN! LET'S GO HOME RIGHT NOW!

WHAT?! WHY ARE YOU HERE?!

GRAB!

NO WAY!

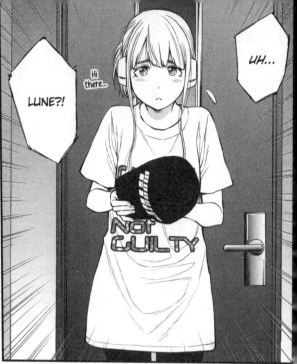

LUNE?!

Hi there...

UH...

Not GUILTY

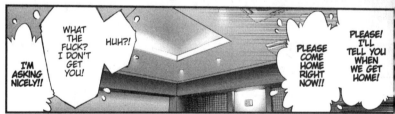

I'M ASKING NICELY!!

WHAT THE FUCK? I DON'T GET YOU!

HUH?!

PLEASE COME HOME RIGHT NOW!!

PLEASE! I'LL TELL YOU WHEN WE GET HOME!

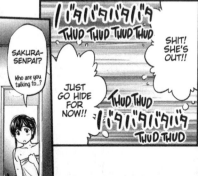

THUD THUD THUD THUD

SHIT! SHE'S OUT!!

SAKURA-SENPAI?

Who are you talking to...?

JUST GO HIDE FOR NOW!!

THUD THUD

THUD THUD THUD THUD

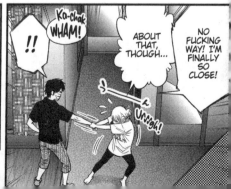

Ka-chak WHAM!

!!

ABOUT THAT, THOUGH...

NO FUCKING WAY! I'M FINALLY SO CLOSE!

Unngh!

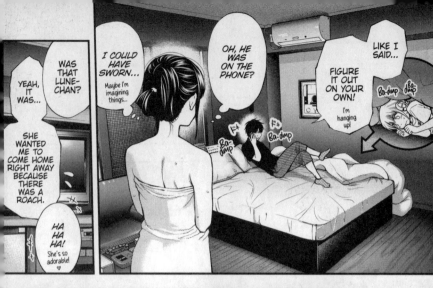

WAS THAT LUNE-CHAN?

YEAH, IT WAS...

SHE WANTED ME TO COME HOME RIGHT AWAY BECAUSE THERE WAS A ROACH.

HA HA HA! She's so adorable! ♡

I COULD HAVE SWORN... Maybe I'm imagining things...

OH, HE WAS ON THE PHONE?

Ba-dump Ba-dump

LIKE I SAID...

FIGURE IT OUT ON YOUR OWN! I'm hanging up!

Ba-dump Ba-dump

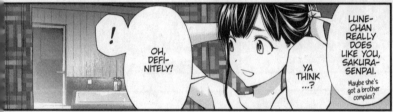

!

OH, DEFINITELY!

YA THINK...?

LUNE-CHAN REALLY DOES LIKE YOU, SAKURA-SENPAI. Maybe she's got a brother complex?

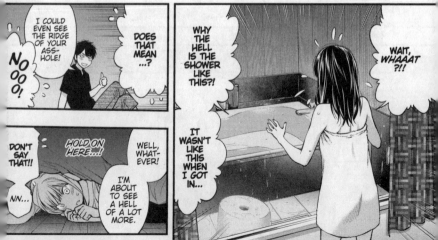

I COULD EVEN SEE THE RIDGE OF YOUR ASSHOLE!

NOOOO!

DOES THAT MEAN...?

DON'T SAY THAT!!

NN...

HOLD ON HERE...!

WELL, WHATEVER! I'M ABOUT TO SEE A HELL OF A LOT MORE.

WHY THE HELL IS THE SHOWER LIKE THIS?!

IT WASN'T LIKE THIS WHEN I GOT IN...

WAIT, WHAAAT?!!

NO ...! Listen...
THIS IS MY FIRST TIME...
DON'T TELL ME...?!
YEAH, YEAH, BE GENTLE. I KNOW!
NN!
BUT I'M RIGHT HERE ...?!
HUFF...
MN...
Shwp Shwp
Smooch Smooch Shuuurp
PANT...
Thw-whp Thw-whp
NN...!
NO...
Thp Thp Thp
くにくに Shwp Shwp
MNNF ...!
AH...
Shwp Shwp Shwp
Tug...
AH...
ANH...
するる、 Sla-slide!

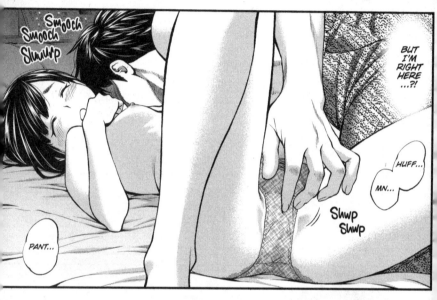

No...
Aaaaanh...
Spreeead
NO...
Squish...
Swf...
THIS IS HOT...
ぱく ぱく
ぱーく
Squish Squish Squish
ぱーく ぱくぱく
Squish Squish Squish
WHAT ARE YOU DOING?!
Stop playing with it!!
IT'S DRIPPING WET...
Spreeead
Tuuug...
AH...
ANH!
Fidget...
Nn...!
......
DON'T SAY THINGS LIKE THAT...
Squish
Swf...

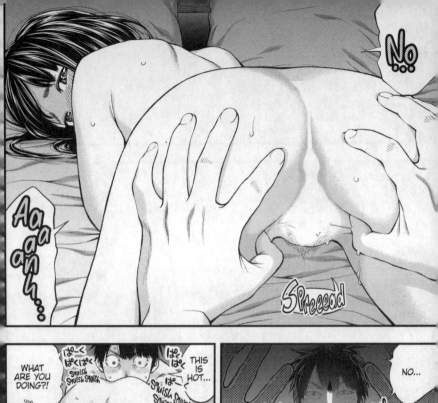

ビクンッ
Quiver!
NN...!
デュラララララララララ
Thwp Thwp Thwp Thwp Thwp Thwpppp!
Huff...
Hn ggh...
ビクッ
Shiver!
ビクッ
Jolt!
Ahh! Ah...!
くり
Thwp
くり
Thwp
Nn...
ビクンッ
Quiver!
Aaanh!
Aaaaaan ggh...
こね
Rub
Rub
こね
Mnnnnn...
まっぎゃ
Rock Hard
THE TIME HAS COME...
ん!!
Huff...
NN...!
ビクッ
Jolt!
Gush...

GRAB
?!
LUNE?!
YOU CAN'T...
Ga-grip...
WHAT DO YOU THINK YOU'RE DOING?!
IF THIS...
FWAP!
HEY...! WHAT?!
WILL SATISFY HIM, THEN...

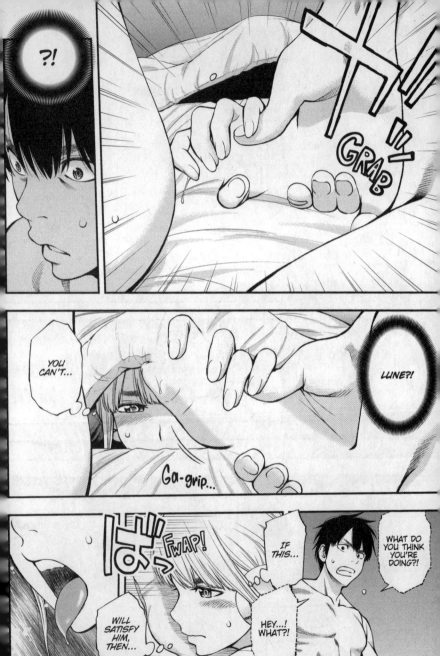

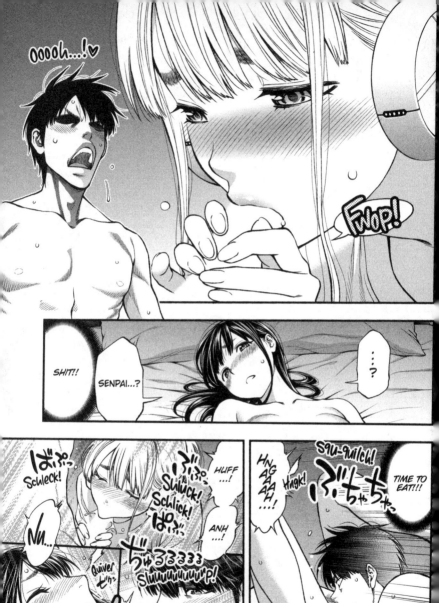

Ooooh...! ♥

FWOP!

SHIT!!

SENPAI...?

...?

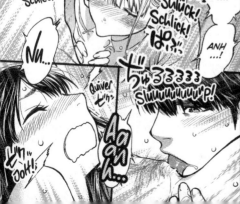

Nn...

Schleck!

HUFF ...!

Schlick! Schlick!

ANH ...!

Quiver twitch

Sluuuuuuuurp!

Agu...

Joll!!

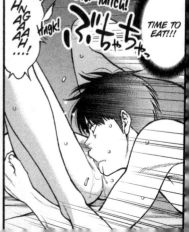

HNG AAAH ....!

Hngk!

SQU-squilch!

TIME TO EAT!!!

Quiver ビクン
Ah! あ
ビクッ Jolt!
Jolt! ビクッ
Ah! あ
Ah!
ビクッ Jolt!
Quiver あ Ah!

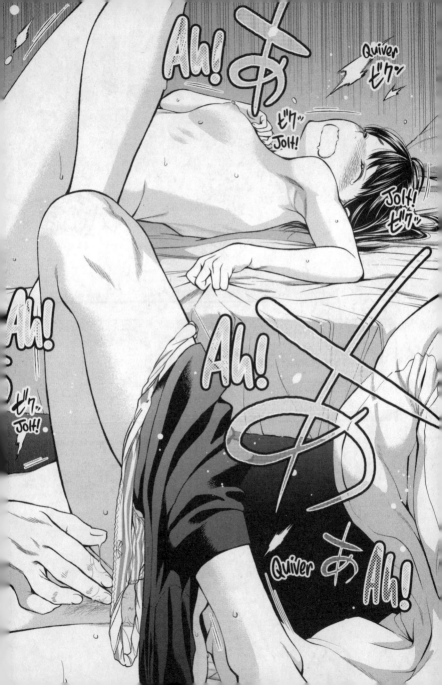

あ Ah!
MNNF ...!
Ah! あ
PFTH...
あ Ah!

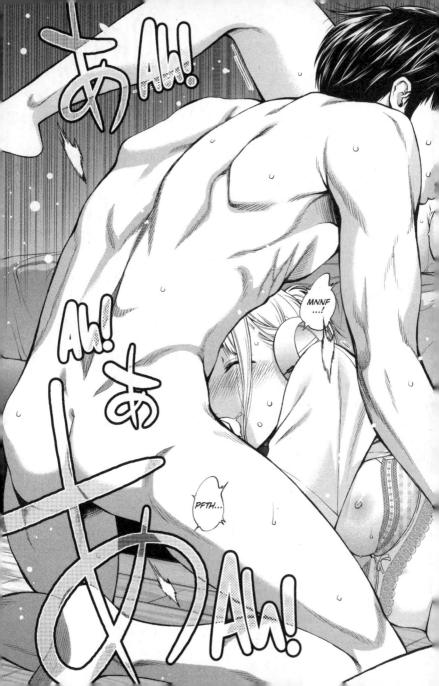

!!
Ungh...!
Thump!
OH NO...
I CAN'T...
DO THIS...

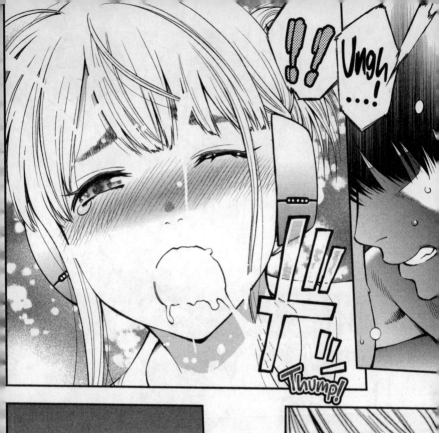

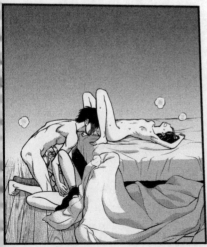

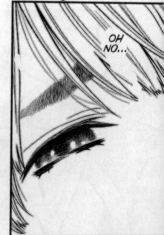

Bmnx!
Uh oh...!
Pai...♥
Sen...

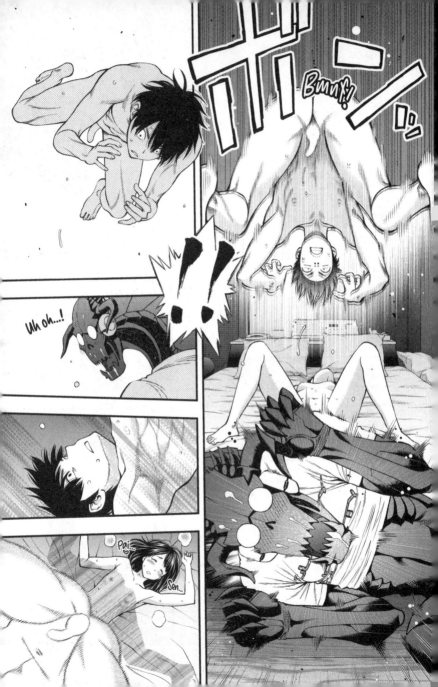

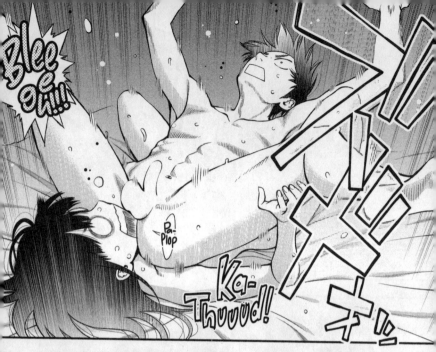

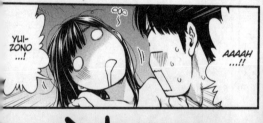

YUI-
ZONO
...!

AAAAH
...!!

OH...

UH...

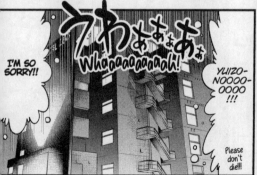

I'M SO
SORRY!!

YUIZO-
NOOOO-
OOOO
!!!

Please
don't
die!!

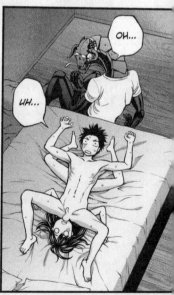

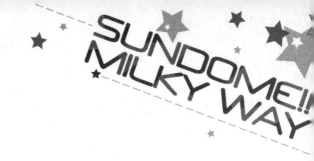

SUNDOME!!
MILKY WAY

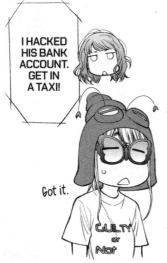

I HACKED HIS BANK ACCOUNT. GET IN A TAXI!

How am I supposed to follow them?

Got it.

GUILTY or Not

Secret Discovery!

Sundome!! Milkyway

Chapter 8 Script Reveal!!

Nooo...!
Spreead
Stop playing with it!!
Hng!
No...!
Spread
You're so fucking wet.
And slippery, too.
Don't say things like that...
Ahn...
Slip
Plip
Ah...
Spreead
Na...!
Ah...
Slirp
Slirp Shlorrrrrrp
Jolt!
Quiver
Quiver
Silk Silk Silk Silk
Ah...
Ah...!
Nn...!
Nn...
Huff...
The time has come...
Jolt!
Pant...
Pant...
Pant!
I never thought that the bath mirror could be a one-way mirror!
Long live one-way mirrors!
The door's unlocked!
The female is in the shower. Now's your chance!
Okay...
Huh?
Ka-Chak
Lune?!
No way!
Ta-
da!
What the fuck? I don't get you!
Huh?!
Please come home with me right now!!
Please! I'll tell you when we get home!
Just go hide for now!!
Shit! She's out!!
Ka-Chak WHAM!
About that, though...
No fucking way! I'm finally so close!
THUD
THUD
THUD
THUD
THUD
Ka-Thuuud!
Splurt!
Spurt!
Splurt!
Ungh...
I can't... do this...
Oh no...
Whoa...?!
Bmmf!
Oh...
Uh...
Aaah...!
Squeeze
Yui-zono...!
Yuizonooooo!!!

Stopping Point
09
Which Will You Choose?!

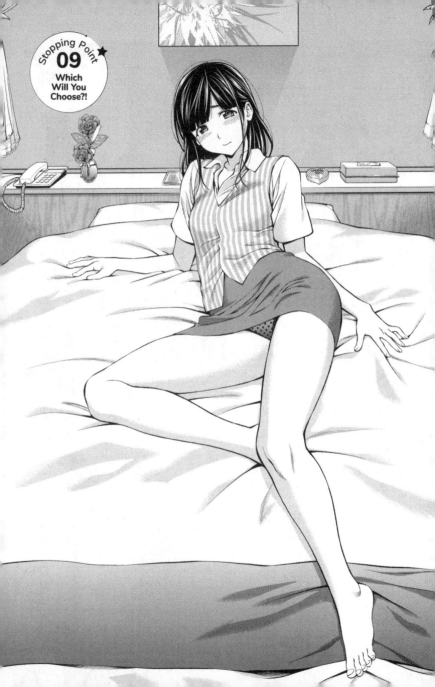

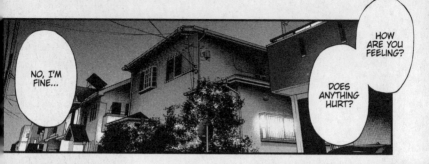

HOW ARE YOU FEELING?

DOES ANYTHING HURT?

NO, I'M FINE...

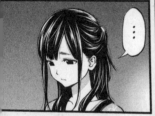

...

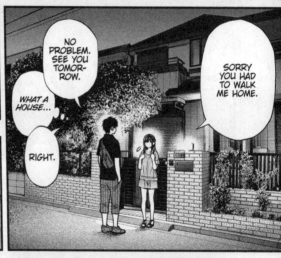

NO PROBLEM. SEE YOU TOMOR-ROW.

WHAT A HOUSE...

RIGHT.

SORRY YOU HAD TO WALK ME HOME.

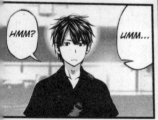

HMM?

UMM...

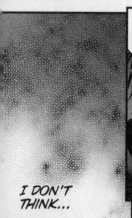

?

I DON'T THINK...

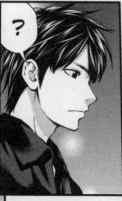

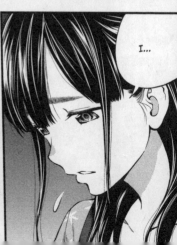

I...

I CAN DO THIS...

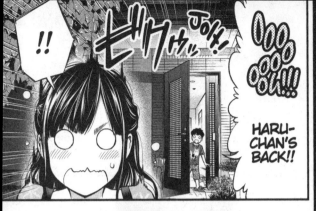
!! ビクッ JOLT!! OOOOH!!!

HARU-CHAN'S BACK!!

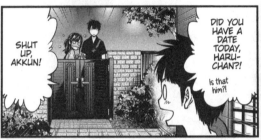
SHUT UP, AKKUN!

DID YOU HAVE A DATE TODAY, HARU-CHAN?!

Is that him?!

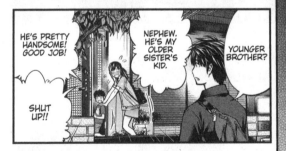
HE'S PRETTY HANDSOME! GOOD JOB!

SHUT UP!!

NEPHEW. HE'S MY OLDER SISTER'S KID.

YOUNGER BROTHER?

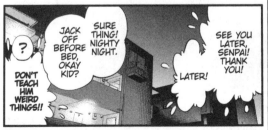
? JACK OFF BEFORE BED, OKAY KID?

SURE THING! NIGHTY NIGHT.

DON'T TEACH HIM WEIRD THINGS!!

SEE YOU LATER, SENPAI! THANK YOU!

LATER!

I...

Ka-Chak...

77

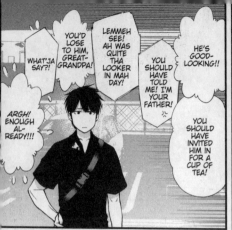

WHAT'JA SAY?!

YOU'D LOSE TO HIM, GREAT-GRANDPA!

LEMMEH SEE! AH WAS QUITE THA LOOKER IN MAH DAY!

YOU SHOULD HAVE TOLD ME! I'M YOUR FATHER!

HE'S GOOD-LOOKING!!

ARGH! ENOUGH AL-READY!!!

YOU SHOULD HAVE INVITED HIM IN FOR A CUP OF TEA!

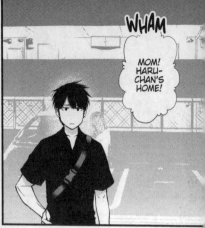

WHAM

MOM! HARU-CHAN'S HOME!

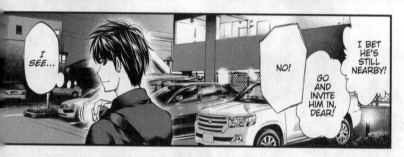

I SEE...

NO!

GO AND INVITE HIM IN, DEAR!

I BET HE'S STILL NEARBY!

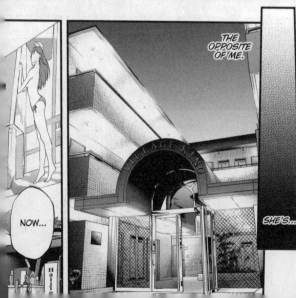

THE OPPOSITE OF ME.

NOW...

SHE'S...

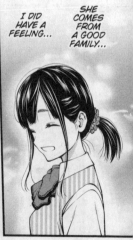

I DID HAVE A FEELING...

SHE COMES FROM A GOOD FAMILY...

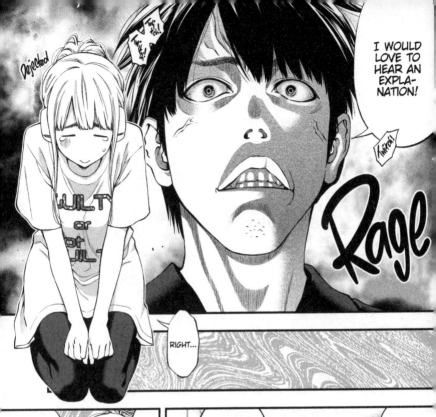

Dejected

Twitch!
Twitch!

I WOULD LOVE TO HEAR AN EXPLANATION!

Twitch!

Rage

RIGHT...

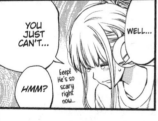

YOU JUST CAN'T...

WELL...

HMM?

Eeep! He's so scary right now...

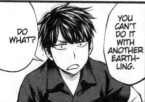

DO WHAT?

YOU CAN'T DO IT WITH ANOTHER EARTHLING.

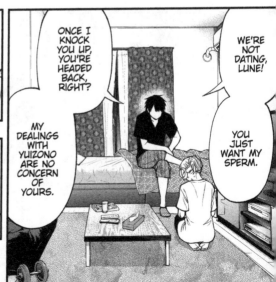

ONCE I KNOCK YOU UP, YOU'RE HEADED BACK, RIGHT?

MY DEALINGS WITH YUIZONO ARE NO CONCERN OF YOURS.

WE'RE NOT DATING, LUNE!

YOU JUST WANT MY SPERM.

79

FOR IT TO WORK...
YOU CAN'T HAVE SEX WITH SOMEONE ELSE BEFORE ME...
IF YOU DO, I FAIL!
HUH?
WAIT, SO...
I HAVE TO BE A VIRGIN?

IF YOU LOSE YOUR VIRGINITY WITH HER...
EVEN IF YOU DO GET ME PREG-NANT...
OUR OFFSPRING WON'T HAVE AN INSATIABLE SEX DRIVE...
THE MISSION WILL BE DECLARED A FAILURE...
AND I'LL BE SENT HOME IN DISGRACE.
WH...
WHAT THE FUCK?
I DIDN'T MEAN TO KEEP IT FROM YOU...
AND...
I KNOW IT'S STRANGE...
BUT...

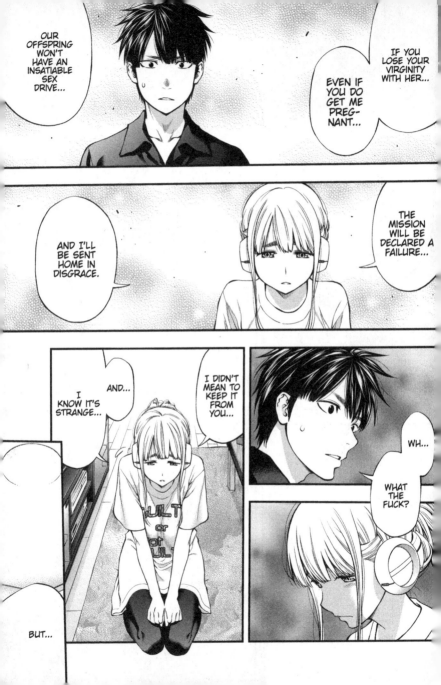

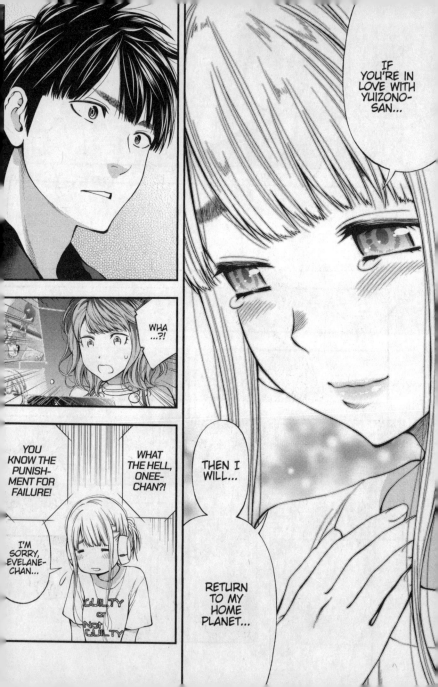

IF YOU'RE IN LOVE WITH YUIZONO-SAN...
THEN I WILL...
RETURN TO MY HOME PLANET...
WHA ...?!
WHAT THE HELL, ONEE-CHAN?!
YOU KNOW THE PUNISHMENT FOR FAILURE!
I'M SORRY, EVELANE-CHAN...
GUILTY or Not GUILTY

I DON'T...
WANT TO BE A BURDEN.
I DON'T WANT TO MAKE YOSHITAKE-SAN...
AND YUIZONO-SAN SUFFER.
SO MAYBE I SHOULD JUST LEAVE...
ONEE-CHAN...
SHE REALLY DOES CARE.
THEN...
THAT'S THE END OF IT!
......
I UNDERSTAND.
OUR TIME TOGETHER WAS BRIEF, BUT STILL, I...

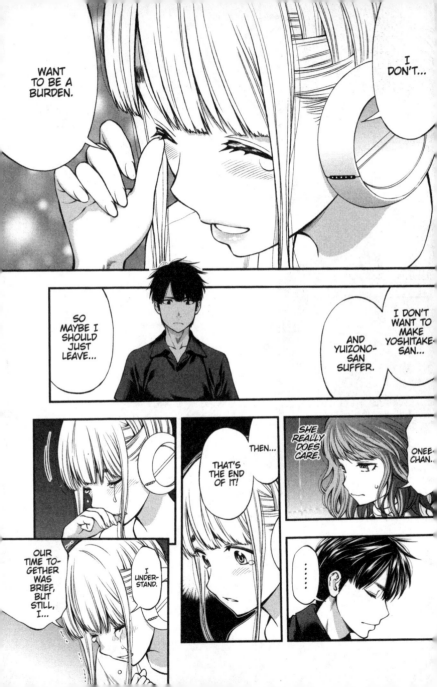

TIME FOR SOME TRAINING!!!
Rock Hard
OOM

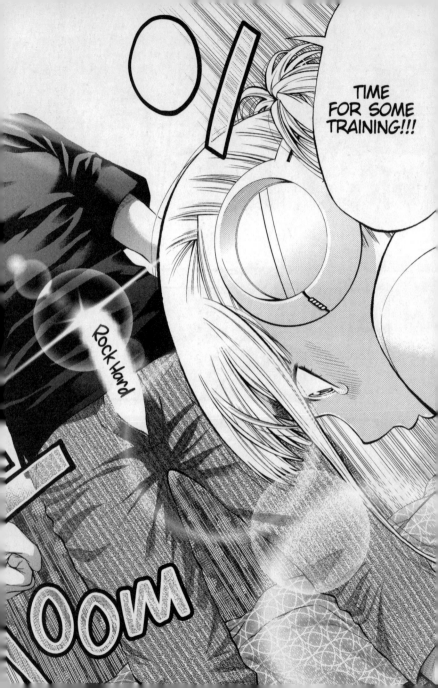

BOO-
STRIP.
NOW.

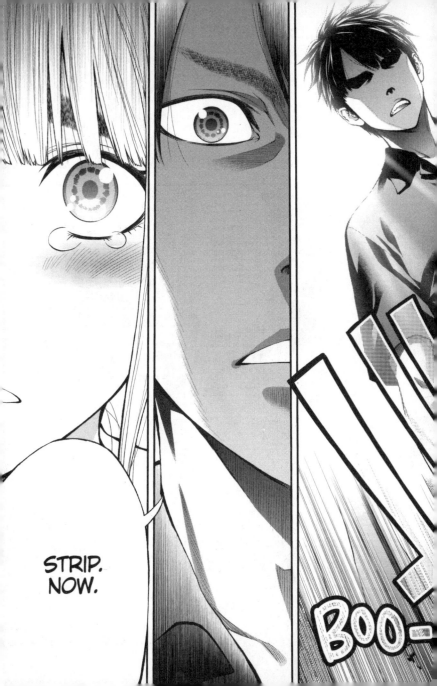

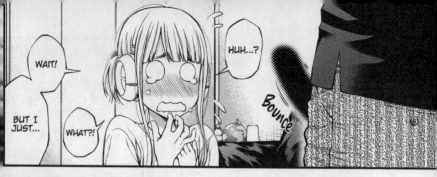

WAIT!

BUT I JUST...

WHAT?!

HUH...?

Bounce

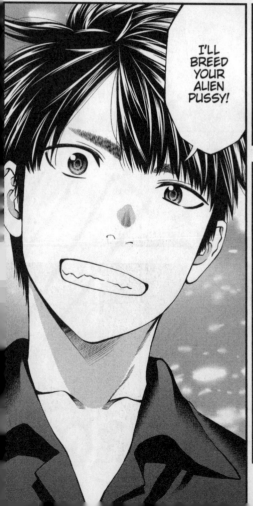

I'LL BREED YOUR ALIEN PUSSY!

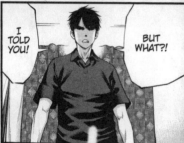

I TOLD YOU!

BUT WHAT?!

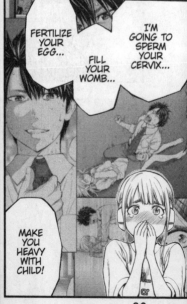

FERTILIZE YOUR EGG...

FILL YOUR WOMB...

I'M GOING TO SPERM YOUR CERVIX...

MAKE YOU HEAVY WITH CHILD!

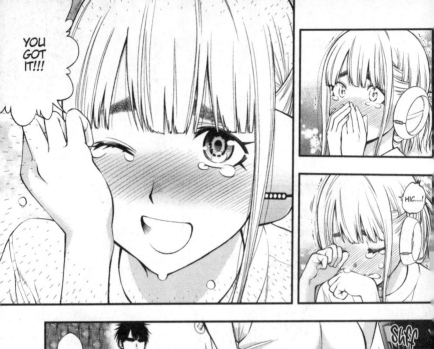

YOU GOT IT!!!

HIC...!

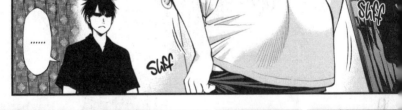

......

Shff

Shff

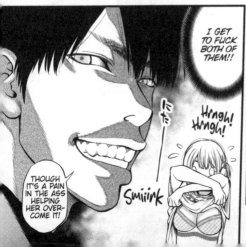

I GET TO FUCK BOTH OF THEM!!

Hrngh! Hrngh!

Smiiink

THOUGH IT'S A PAIN IN THE ASS HELPING HER OVERCOME IT!

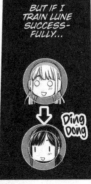

BUT IF I TRAIN LUNE SUCCESSFULLY...

Ding Dong

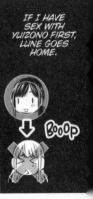

IF I HAVE SEX WITH YUIZONO FIRST, LUNE GOES HOME.

Booop

HUH?!
WHAT?!
WHY ARE WE ON THE BALCONY...?
DON'T HIDE YOUR NIPPLES! STICK THEM OUT OVER THE EDGE!
HUH?!
WHAAAAT?!
LIKE THIS...?
ぐい SHOVE
MORE!
WHAT...
ぐい SHOVE
Hnnngh...
ぽよよよ~ん Boi-yoi-yoi-yoing
NOW EVERYONE OUTSIDE CAN SEE...
Swf...

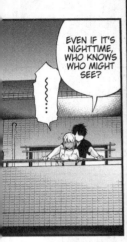

EVEN IF IT'S NIGHTTIME, WHO KNOWS WHO MIGHT SEE?

......!

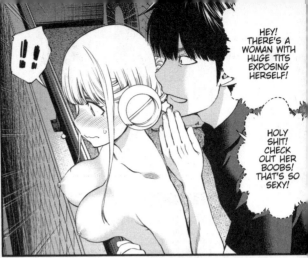

!!

HEY! THERE'S A WOMAN WITH HUGE TITS EXPOSING HERSELF!

HOLY SHIT! CHECK OUT HER BOOBS! THAT'S SO SEXY!

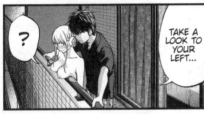

?

TAKE A LOOK TO YOUR LEFT...

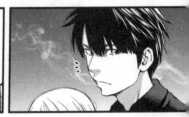

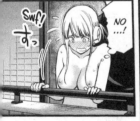

Swf!

NO ...!

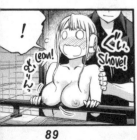

!

Leon!

Shove!

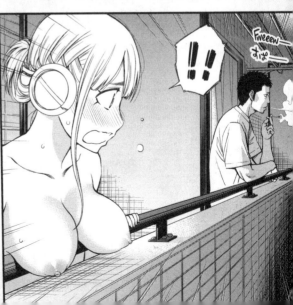

!!

Fwweeew

89

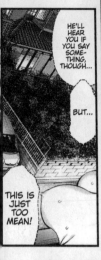

HE'LL HEAR YOU IF YOU SAY SOMETHING, THOUGH...

BUT...

THIS IS JUST TOO MEAN!

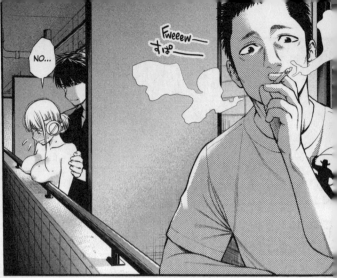

NO...

Fweeew— すぱ—

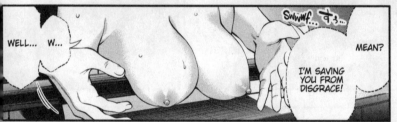

WELL... W...

Swwwf... すぅ...

MEAN?

I'M SAVING YOU FROM DISGRACE!

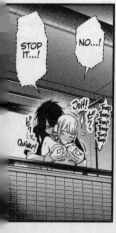

STOP IT...!

NO...!

JoH! ビクッ Quiver!

Trmp Trmp Trmp Trmp Trmp Trmp Trmp Trmp

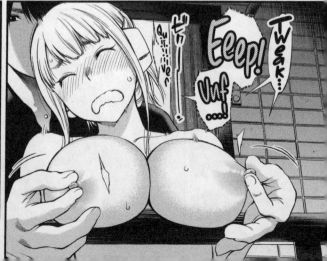

Quiiiiiver!

Eeep!

Tweak...

Vnf ぐっ

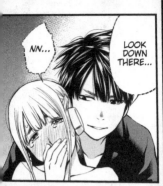

NN...

LOOK DOWN THERE...

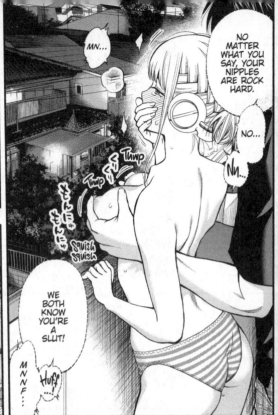

MN...

NO MATTER WHAT YOU SAY, YOUR NIPPLES ARE ROCK HARD.

NO...

NN...

Thwp Thwp Thwp

SQUISH SQUISH

WE BOTH KNOW YOU'RE A SLUT!

MNNF...

Huff!...

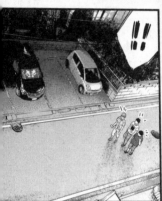

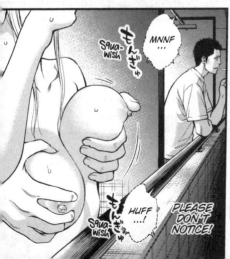

MNNF...

SQUA-WISH

HUFF...!

SQUA-WISH

PLEASE DON'T NOTICE!

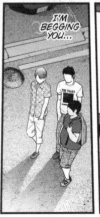

I'M BEGGING YOU...

PLEASE DON'T LOOK UP...

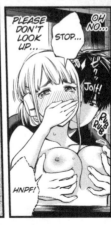

STOP...

OH NO...

Jolt!

PLEASE DON'T LOOK UP...

HNPF!

I'M GONNA TRANSFORM...!

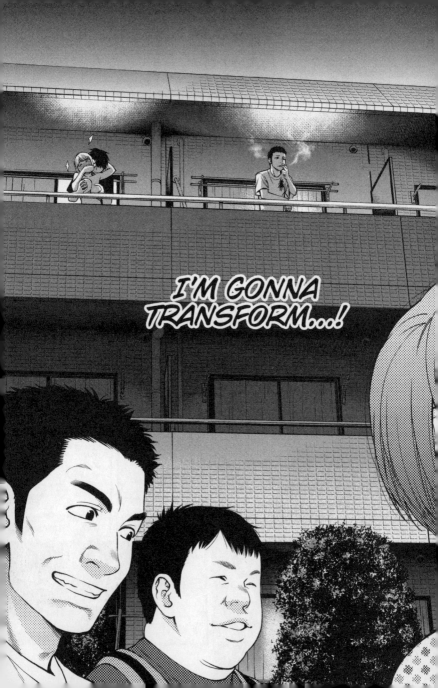

Hufffffff...
ビクッ
JOLT!
ビクンッ
Quiver!
ビク…ッ
Quiver

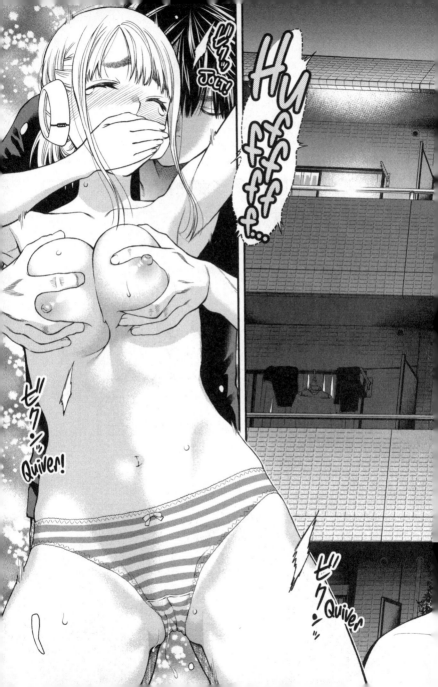

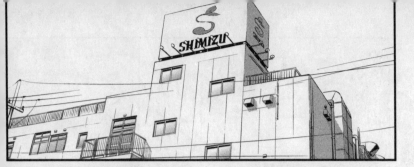

は ~ siiiiiiii
...iiiigh...

UGH...

YOU LOOK DEAD ON YOUR FEET.

WHAT'S THE MATTER, HARUKA?

NO! IT'S NOTHING... Umm...

WHOA, WHAT THE HELL?!

KA-KLATTER
ガタタッ

MIKA-SAN!!

HMM. IS THIS ABOUT SAKURA?

What did he do?

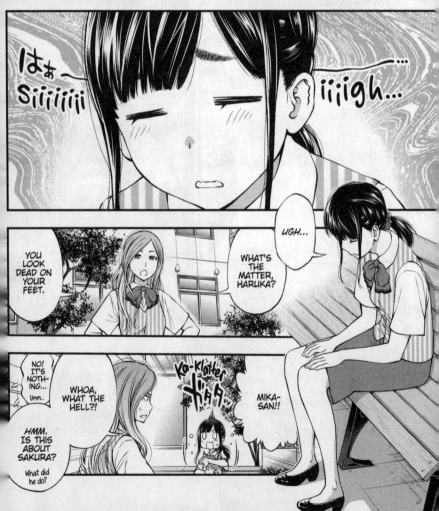

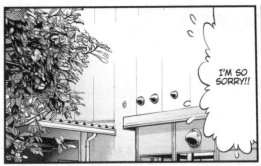

I'M SO SORRY!!

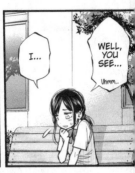

I....

WELL, YOU SEE...

Uhmm...

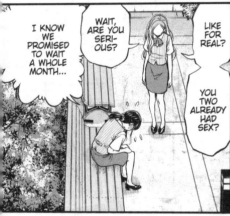

I KNOW WE PROMISED TO WAIT A WHOLE MONTH...

WAIT, ARE YOU SERI- OUS?

LIKE FOR REAL?

YOU TWO ALREADY HAD SEX?

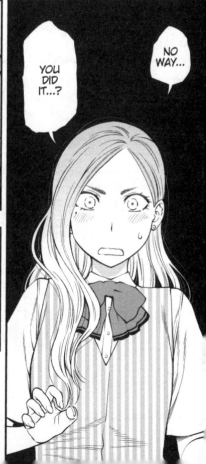

YOU DID IT...?

NO WAY...

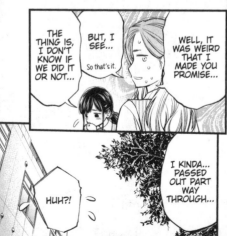

THE THING IS, I DON'T KNOW IF WE DID IT OR NOT...

BUT, I SEE...

So that's it.

WELL, IT WAS WEIRD THAT I MADE YOU PROMISE...

I KINDA... PASSED OUT PART WAY THROUGH...

HUH?!

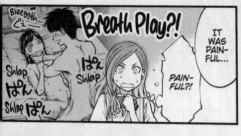

Breath Play?!

Bleegoth...

Shlop
Shlop

IT WAS PAINFUL...

PAINFUL?!

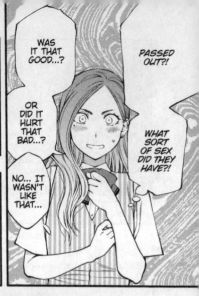

WAS IT THAT GOOD...?

PASSED OUT?!

OR DID IT HURT THAT BAD...?

WHAT SORT OF SEX DID THEY HAVE?!

NO... IT WASN'T LIKE THAT...

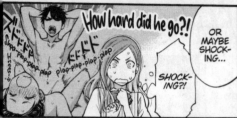

How hard did he go?!

OR MAYBE SHOCKING...

SHOCKING?!

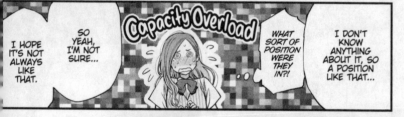

Capacity Overload

I HOPE IT'S NOT ALWAYS LIKE THAT.

SO YEAH, I'M NOT SURE...

WHAT SORT OF POSITION WERE THEY IN?!

I DON'T KNOW ANYTHING ABOUT IT, SO A POSITION LIKE THAT...

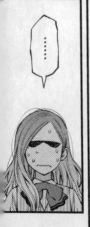

......

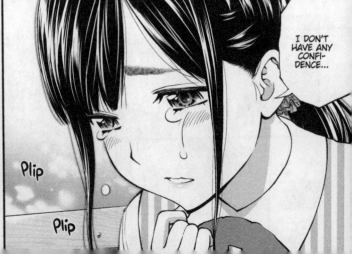

I DON'T HAVE ANY CONFIDENCE...

Plip

Plip

SHIMIZU
SAAAAAAAAAAA...
KUUUUUUUUUUUUU...
RAAAAAAAAAAAA!!!
WHA-BLAM
CRUMBLE
CRUMBLE
......
WHAT THE FUCK IS YOUR PROBLEM?!
WHAT DID YOU DO TO HER?!
WHEN?!
I HEARD YOU CHOKED HER AND USED WEIRD POSI-TIONS!!
......
Uhmm...

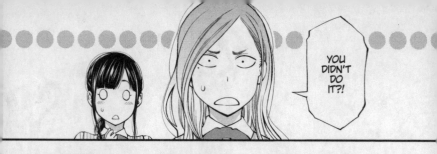

YOU DIDN'T DO IT?!

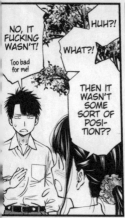

NO, IT FUCKING WASN'T!

Too bad for me!

HUH?!

WHAT?!

THEN IT WASN'T SOME SORT OF POSITION??

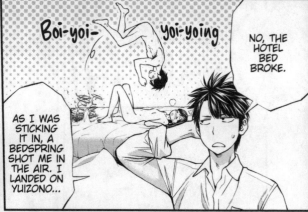

Boi-yoi- yoi-yoing

NO, THE HOTEL BED BROKE.

AS I WAS STICKING IT IN, A BEDSPRING SHOT ME IN THE AIR. I LANDED ON YUIZONO...

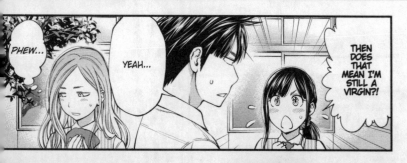

PHEW...

YEAH...

THEN DOES THAT MEAN I'M STILL A VIRGIN?!

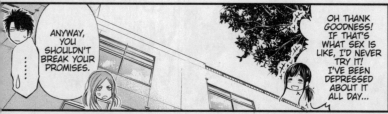

ANYWAY, YOU SHOULDN'T BREAK YOUR PROMISES.

OH THANK GOODNESS! IF THAT'S WHAT SEX IS LIKE, I'D NEVER TRY IT! I'VE BEEN DEPRESSED ABOUT IT ALL DAY...

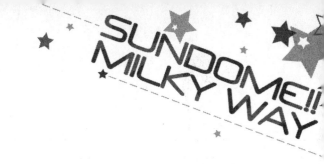

I really
shouldn't
have
punched
that
concrete...

Shiver
Shiver

Shiver

Secret Discovery!

Sundome!! Milkyway

Chapter 9 Script Reveal!!

I can do this...
Ooooooo oh!!!
Haru-chan's back!!
Jooolt!
You went on your date today, didn't you, Haru-chan?!
Is that him?!
Shut up, Aikun!
Younger brother?
Nephew. He's my older sister's kid.
He's pretty handsome! Good job!
See you later, Senpai! Thank you
How are you feeling?
Does anything hurt?
Peaceful, quiet neighborhood
No, I'm fine...
Sorry you had to walk me home...
No problem. See you tomorrow.
...
Right...
Umm...
Hmm?
?
I don't think...
If you're in love with Yuizono-san...
I don't...
want to be a burden.
I don't want to make Yoshitake-san...
and Yuizono-san suffer.
So maybe I should just leave...
Wha...?!
Onee-chan...
She really does care.
Then...
that's the end of it!
I understand...
What the hell, Onee-chan?!
You know the punishment for failure!
...
I'm sorry, Levelane-chan...
then I...
will go home to my planet...
Huh...?
But what?!
I told you!
I'll breed your alien pussy!
I'm going to sperm your cervix...
fertilize your egg...
and make you heavy with child!
fill your womb...
Flashback
Hic...!
Plip Plip Plip
Skf Skf
If I have sex with Yuizono first, Lune goes home.
Before
After
But if I train Lune successfully...
I get to fuck both of them!! Hnngh! Hnngh!
Before
After

THIS IS YOUR FIRST TIME, LUNE-CHAN?!
Stopping Point 10
THAT'S RIGHT!
I'M EXCITED!
SO, WHERE ARE YOU FROM AGAIN? SAITAMA? GUNMA?
Nowhere with a beach...
WELL...
WHY THE FUCK AM I DRIVING?
SHUT THE HELL UP, SALES! IT'S THREE AGAINST ONE.
OH! LOOK! WE CAN SEE IT NOW!
OH, WOW!

Stopping Point 10
Summer, Abalone, and Aliens
THE BEACH!!

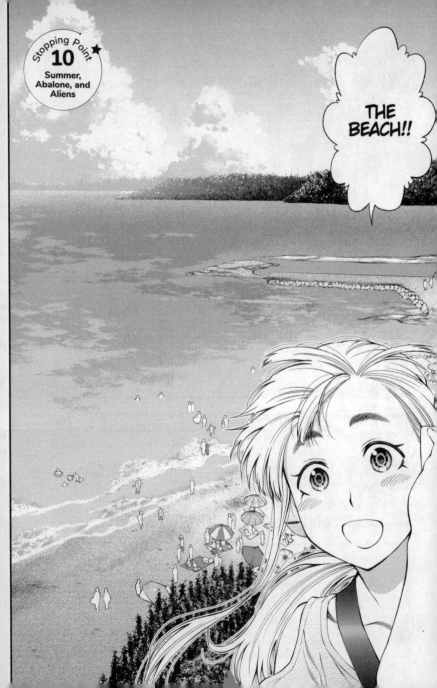

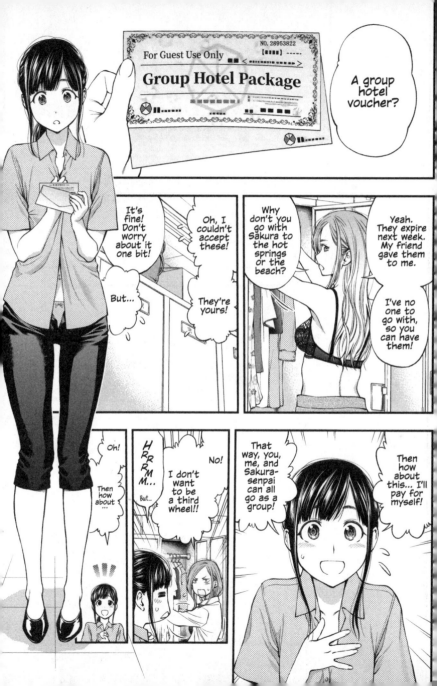

NO. 28953822

For Guest Use Only

Group Hotel Package

A group hotel voucher?

It's fine! Don't worry about it one bit!

Oh, I couldn't accept these!

But...

They're yours!

Why don't you go with Sakura to the hot springs or the beach?

Yeah. They expire next week. My friend gave them to me.

I've no one to go with, so you can have them!

Oh!

Then how about...

HRRRM...

But...

I don't want to be a third wheel!!

No!

That way, you, me, and Sakura-senpai can all go as a group!

Then how about this... I'll pay for myself!

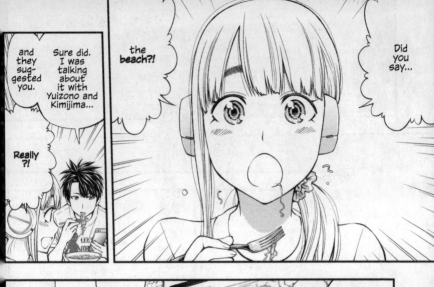

and they suggested you.

Sure did. I was talking about it with Yuizono and Kimijima...

the beach?!

Did you say...

Really?!

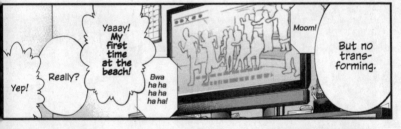

Yaaay! My first time at the beach!

Really?

Yep!

Bwa ha ha ha ha ha ha!

Moom!

But no transforming.

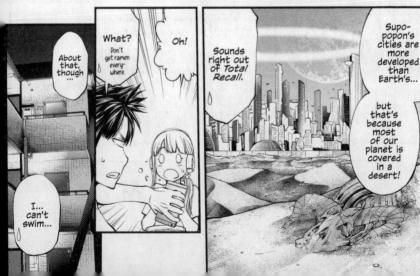

About that, though...

What? Don't get ramen every-where.

Oh!

I... can't swim...

Sounds right out of *Total Recall*.

Supopopon's cities are more developed than Earth's...

but that's because most of our planet is covered in a desert!

THANKS FOR WAITING!
......
THOSE CLOTHES ARE IN THE WAY!
THIS IS TECHNICALLY A BATHING SUIT, BUT IT'S DESIGNED TO WEAR WHENEVER!
It's trendy!

SUN-SCREEN IS ESSENTIAL!!
UNTIE THOSE BRAS AND SIT DOWN HERE!!
I SHALL ENSURE EVERY SINGLE PART OF ALL THREE OF YOU IS COATED!!
Spluuurt
I WILL END YOU!
NO THANK YOU!
You'll make it weird!
......
ふ――
Huff!
ふ――…
Huuu fffff...
ふぅぅぅうううううううう うううううぅ…
Huuuu ufffff...
Wheeeze
Wheeeze
Wheeeze
Cha-ching

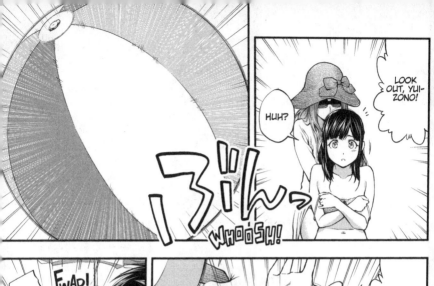

LOOK OUT, YUI-ZONO!

HUH?

ぶん
WHOOSH!

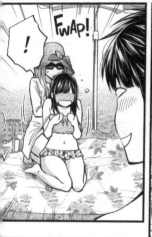

FWAP!

!

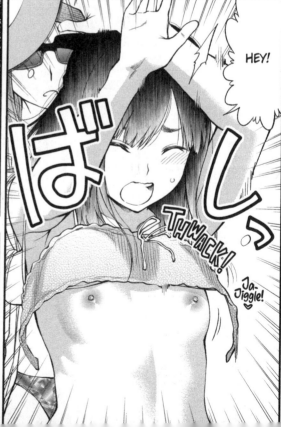

HEY!

ばし
THWACK!

Ja-Jiggle!

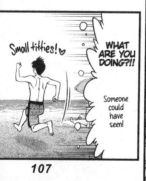

Small titties! ♥

WHAT ARE YOU DOING?!!

Someone could have seen!

107

Don't forget your head-phones!
They're water-proof! ♪
It's salty!
This really is her first time.
Seriously?
JOLT!
Slurp Slurp
Quiver
What's the matter?
Where is that idiot?
Fidget
Fidget

ぶんっ
WHOOSH!
Hey! Watch what you're doing!
WHA-WHOOSH
ぶんぶん
WHOOSH!
ぶんっ
Mika-san!
Swing it more!
Oh no!
ぶ!
Pffffffwwwth!
What the heck are you doing?!
You got a big one.
Giggle Giggle

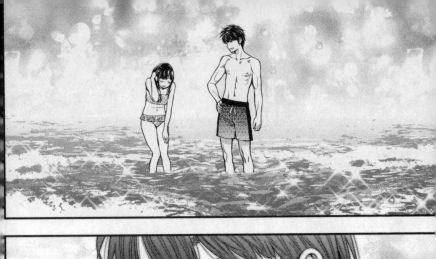

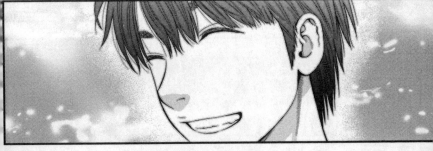

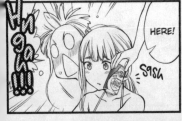

HU GA!!!

HERE!

SSH

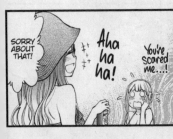

SORRY ABOUT THAT!

Aha ha ha!

You're scared me...!

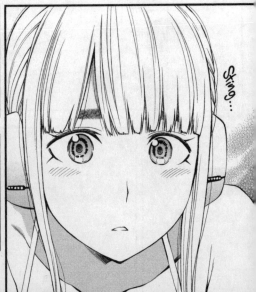

Sting...

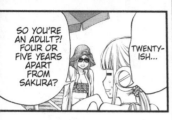

SO YOU'RE AN ADULT?! FOUR OR FIVE YEARS APART FROM SAKURA?

TWENTY-ISH...

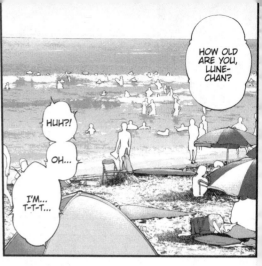

HOW OLD ARE YOU, LUNE-CHAN?

HUH?!

OH...

I'M... T-T-T...

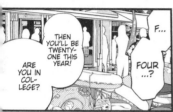

THEN YOU'LL BE TWENTY-ONE THIS YEAR!

ARE YOU IN COLLEGE?

F...

FOUR...?

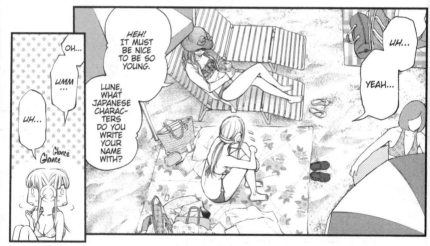

OH...

UMM...

UH...

Glance Glance

HEH! IT MUST BE NICE TO BE SO YOUNG.

LUNE, WHAT JAPANESE CHARACTERS DO YOU WRITE YOUR NAME WITH?

UH...

YEAH...

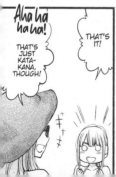

Aha ha ha ha!

THAT'S JUST KATAKANA, THOUGH!

THAT'S IT!

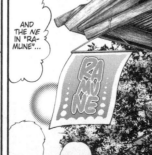

AND THE NE IN "RAMUNE"...

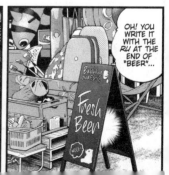

OH! YOU WRITE IT WITH THE RU AT THE END OF "BEER"...

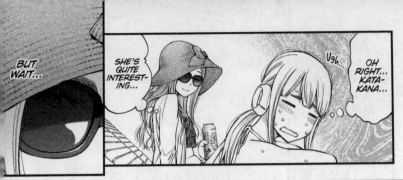

BUT WAIT...

SHE'S QUITE INTERESTING...

Ugh...

OH RIGHT... KATAKANA...

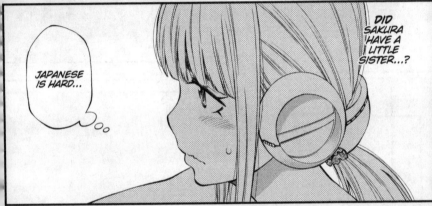

JAPANESE IS HARD...

DID SAKURA HAVE A LITTLE SISTER...?

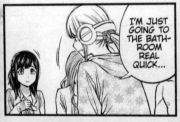

I'M JUST GOING TO THE BATHROOM REAL QUICK...

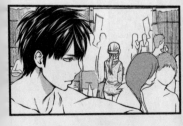

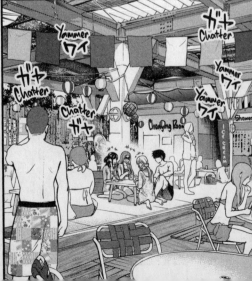

Yammer ワイ

Chatter ガヤ

Chatter ガヤ

Chatter ガヤ

Yammer ワイ

Yammer ワイ

Changing Room

Shower

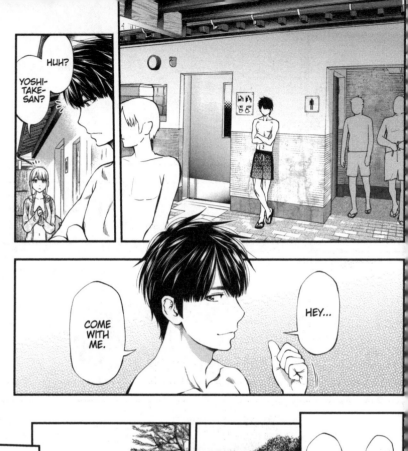

HUH?

YOSHI-
TAKE-
SAN?

COME
WITH
ME.

HEY...

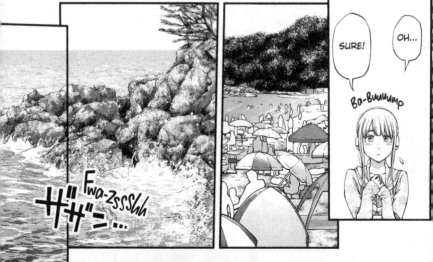

SURE!

OH...

Ba-Buuump

Fwa-Zssshh

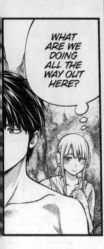

WHAT ARE WE DOING ALL THE WAY OUT HERE?

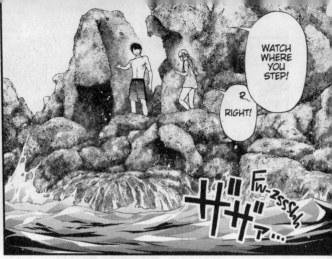

WATCH WHERE YOU STEP!

R... RIGHT!

Fw-zssshh...

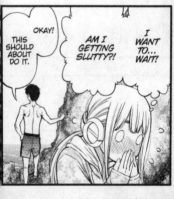

OKAY! THIS SHOULD ABOUT DO IT.

AM I GETTING SLUTTY?!

I WANT TO... WAIT!

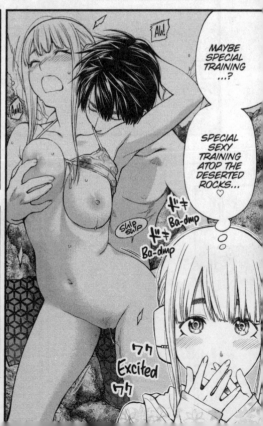

Ah!

MAYBE SPECIAL TRAINING...?

SPECIAL SEXY TRAINING ATOP THE DESERTED ROCKS... ♡

Ah!

Ah!

Slip Slip

Ba-dmp

Ba-dmp

Excited

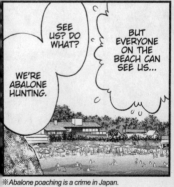

SEE US? DO WHAT?

BUT EVERYONE ON THE BEACH CAN SEE US...

WE'RE ABALONE HUNTING.

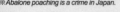

※ Abalone poaching is a crime in Japan.

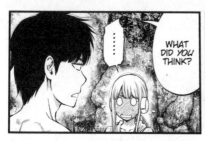

WHAT DID *YOU* THINK?

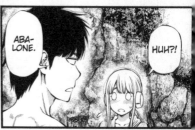

ABA-LONE.

HUH?!

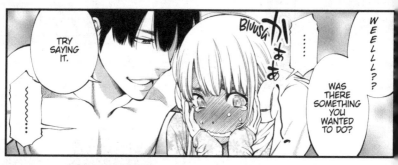

TRY SAYING IT.

WEELLL?? BluuSh

WAS THERE SOMETHING YOU WANTED TO DO?

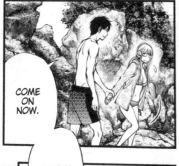

COME ON NOW.

I LOVE ABALONE!

YOU'RE LYING!

IT'S NOT A LIE! I actually do!

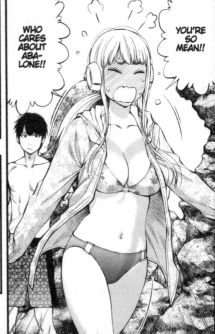

WHO CARES ABOUT ABA-LONE!!

YOU'RE SO MEAN!!

I ESPECIALLY LOVE THE ABALONE...
BETWEEN A WOMAN'S LEGS!!
Like this!!
Hngah!!
Yoooiiinnk!
No...
Schlurp urp-urp-urp-urp-urp-urp!
DON'T BE SO ROUGH...
MNNF ...!
RUB RUB RUB RUB RUB RUB RUB RUB

I'LL TRANS-FORM...
ANH...
ぬちゃ ぬちゃ ぬちゃ ぬちゃ
Sqlch sqlch sqlch sqlch
Quiver!
ビクッ Jolt!
HN-GAH!
ぐちゅ Shlirk
ぐちゅ Shlirk
ぐちゅ Shlirk
ぐちゅ Shlirk
AAANH!
AH...!
ビクン Jolt!
SAY IT.
YOU WANTED TRAINING, DIDN'T YOU?
!
NO!
Mun...
ビクッ Jolt!
TELL THE TRUTH AND I'LL REWARD YOU!
LIE, AND I STOP.
......
......
....
UGH...

I DID...
Bluuuuush!
I WANTED TRAIN-ING...
THAT'S MY GIRL!
Rock Hard
Fwa-whiiip
YOUR TREAT IS MY COCK!
A SLUTTY REWARD FOR SLUTTY LUNE!
......
OH...
NO...
WHEN...
DID I START TO...

WHEN DID I BECOME A SLUT?
I WANT HIM TO TOUCH MY BODY...
AND I WANT TO TOUCH HIS...
AM I JEALOUS...?
OH NO...
I CAN'T STOP...
I WANT MORE...
GULP
AND I WANT TO DO MORE...
AH...

I LOVE THIS.
Kanoya

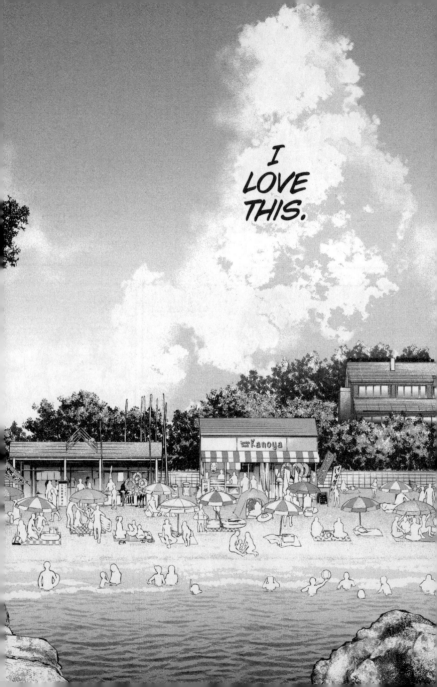

Splup!
NN!
Schluck!
Squelch
MNNF ...!

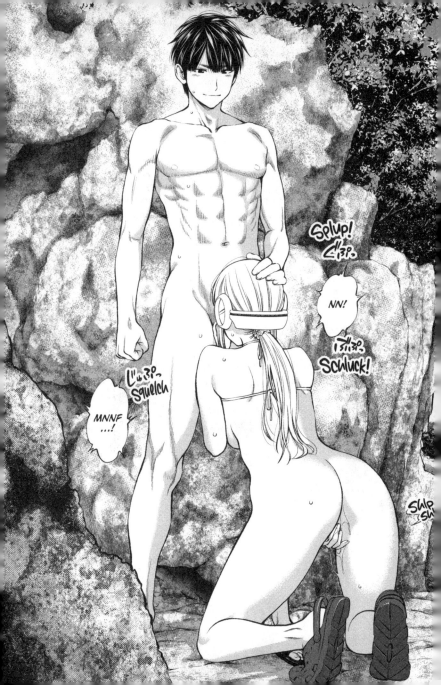

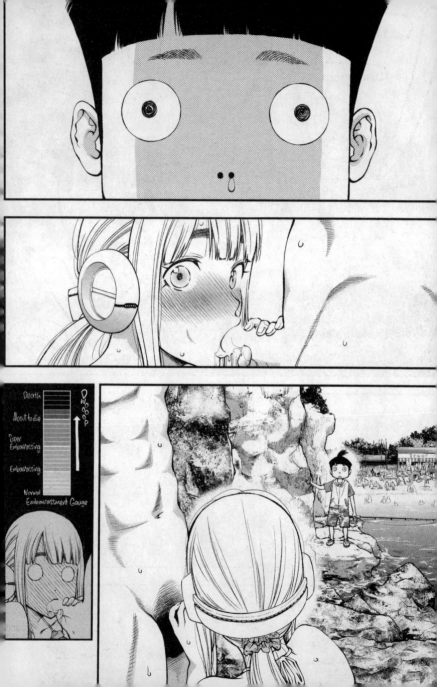

Death

About to die

Super
Embarrassing

Embarrassing

Normal
Embarrassment Gauge

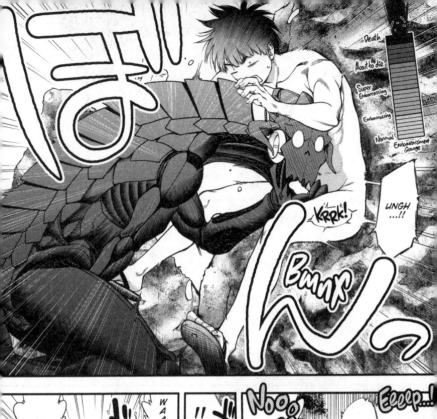

Death

About to die

Super Embarrassing

Embarrassing

Normal | Embarrassment Gauge

KRRK!

UNGH ...!!

BMMF

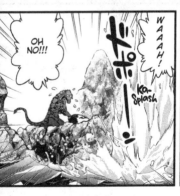

OH NO!!!

WAAAH!

Ka-Splash!

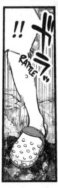

!!

RATTLE

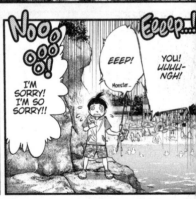

NOOOOOOO!

EEEP...!

I'M SORRY! I'M SO SORRY!!

EEEP!

Monster—

YOU! UUUU-NGH!

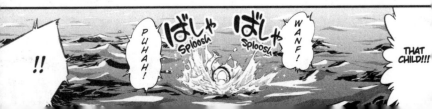

!!

PUHAH!

SPLOOSH

SPLOOSH

WANF!

THAT CHILD!!!

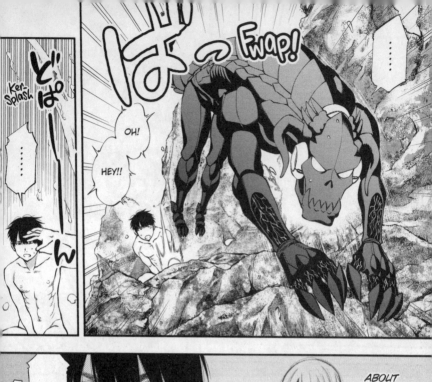

Ker-Splash

ど！ば！
ん

OH!

HEY!!

Fwap!

． ． ．

． ． ．

． ． ．

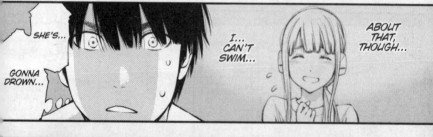

SHE'S...

GONNA DROWN...

I... CAN'T SWIM...

ABOUT THAT, THOUGH...

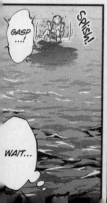

GASP ....!

Splish!

WAIT...

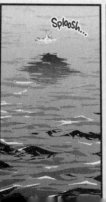

Sploosh...

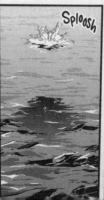

Sploosh

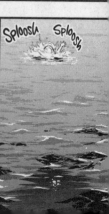

Sploosh   Sploosh

HER FEET MUST TOUCH THE BOTTOM!!
PAAANT!
PAAANT!
Streeeeech!
JEEZ!
Fwap!
ばっ
ごぽぽ…
Blub-a-blub
LET ME IN!
YOSHI-TAKE-SAN!
YOU GO HIDE BY THE ROCKS!

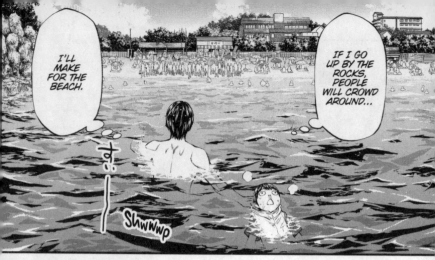

I'LL MAKE FOR THE BEACH.

IF I GO UP BY THE ROCKS, PEOPLE WILL CROWD AROUND...

ShwwwP

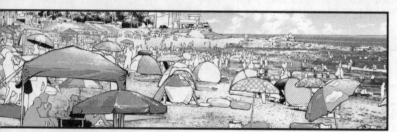

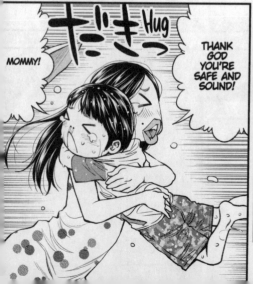

Hug

MOMMY!

THANK GOD YOU'RE SAFE AND SOUND!

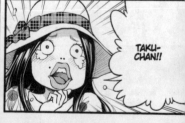

TAKU-CHAN!!

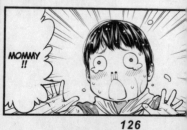

MOMMY!!

126

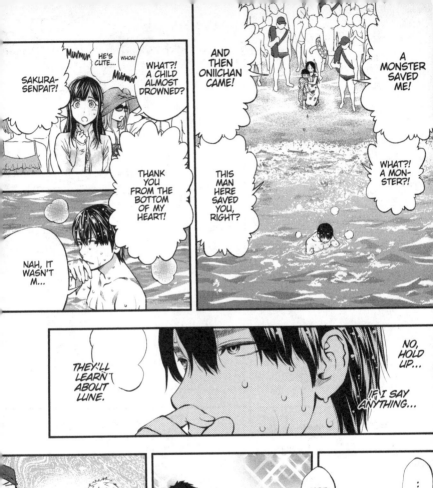

SAKURA-SENPAI?!

Mur mur

HE'S CUTE...

WHOA!

Mur mur

WHAT?! A CHILD ALMOST DROWNED?

AND THEN ONIICHAN CAME!

A MONSTER SAVED ME!

THANK YOU FROM THE BOTTOM OF MY HEART!

THIS MAN HERE SAVED YOU, RIGHT?

WHAT?! A MONSTER?!

NAH, IT WASN'T M...

THEY'LL LEARN ABOUT LUNE.

NO, HOLD UP...

IF I SAY ANYTHING...

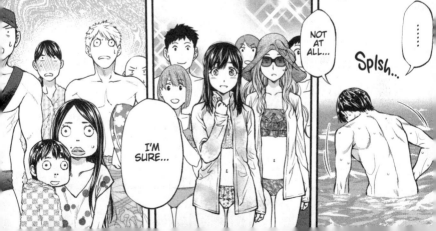

NOT AT ALL...

·····

SPlsh...

I'M SURE...

ANYONE WOULD DO WHAT I DID!!
Rock Hard
PERVERT!!!
SENPAI! LOOK DOWN!
WHAT THE HELL?!
WHY THE HELL ARE YOU HARD?!
HUH?!
ギャー
Screeech!
わ
Whoa!
DICK MIS-SILE!
キャー
Eeeek!

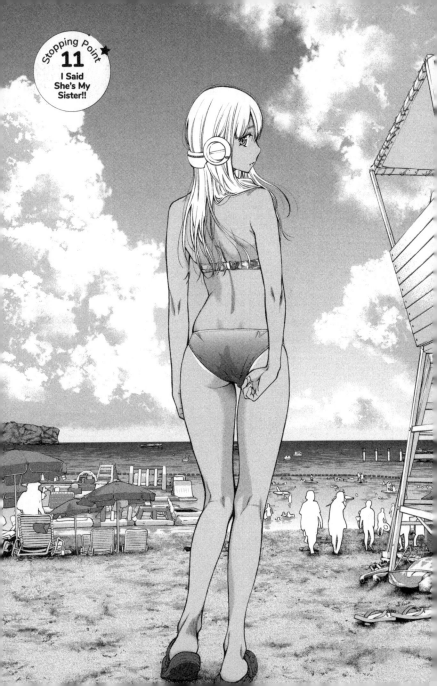

Stopping Point
★
11
I Said
She's My
Sister!!

WOW!
IT'S SO PRETTY!
KRSH-SHHH-SHAAA-AAA-AAA
パチ Crackle
パチ Crackle

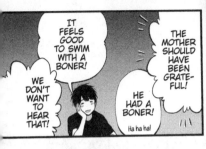

IT FEELS GOOD TO SWIM WITH A BONER!

WE DON'T WANT TO HEAR THAT!

HE HAD A BONER!

THE MOTHER SHOULD HAVE BEEN GRATEFUL!

Ha ha ha!

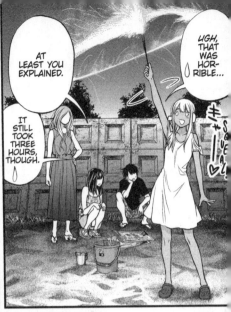

AT LEAST YOU EXPLAINED.

IT STILL TOOK THREE HOURS, THOUGH.

UGH, THAT WAS HORRIBLE...

SQUEAL!

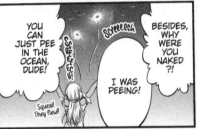

YOU CAN JUST PEE IN THE OCEAN, DUDE!

SCREECH!

Skreeech

BESIDES, WHY WERE YOU NAKED?!

I WAS PEEING!

Squeal! They flew!!

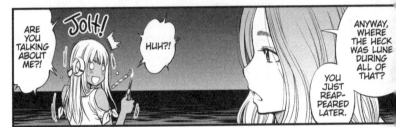

ARE YOU TALKING ABOUT ME?!

JOH!

HUH?!

ANYWAY, WHERE THE HECK WAS LUNE DURING ALL OF THAT?

YOU JUST REAPPEARED LATER.

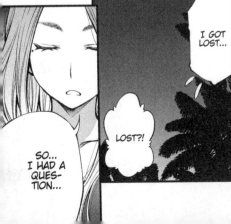

SO... I HAD A QUESTION...

I GOT LOST...

UHMM...

LOST?!

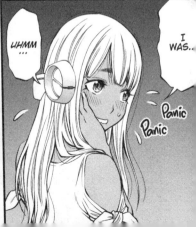

I WAS..

Panic
Panic

DID YOU ALWAYS HAVE A SISTER, SAKURA?
YOU'VE NEVER MENTIONED HER.
ND YOU IO LOOK OTHING ALIKE.
MIKA-SAN...? WHAT ARE YOU SAYING ...?
......
UNE AS...

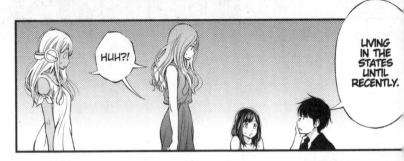

HUH?!

LIVING IN THE STATES UNTIL RECENTLY.

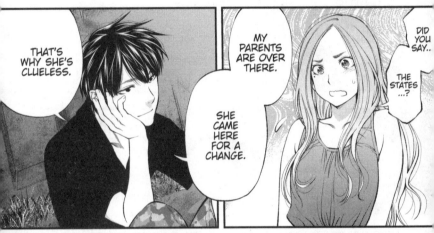

THAT'S WHY SHE'S CLUELESS.

MY PARENTS ARE OVER THERE.

SHE CAME HERE FOR A CHANGE.

DID YOU SAY..

THE STATES...?

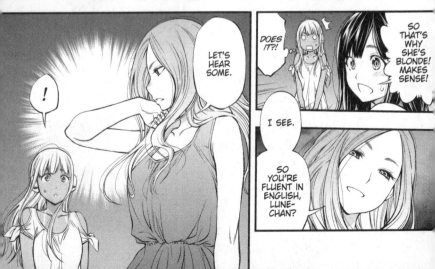

LET'S HEAR SOME.

!

DOES IT?!

SO THAT'S WHY SHE'S BLONDE! MAKES SENSE!

I SEE.

SO YOU'RE FLUENT IN ENGLISH, LUNE-CHAN?

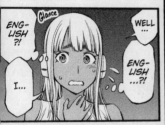

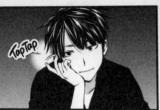

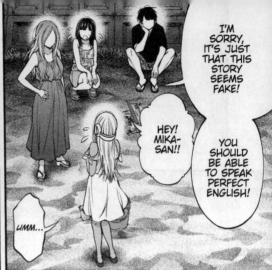

I'M SORRY, IT'S JUST THAT THIS STORY SEEMS FAKE!
YOU SHOULD BE ABLE TO SPEAK PERFECT ENGLISH!
HEY! MIKA-SAN!!
UMM...
WELL...
ENG-LISH...?!
Glance
ENG-LISH?!
I...
TapTap
OH RIGHT...!
Click
Click Click Click Click
English
<I APOLOGIZE FOR MY STRANGE BEHAVIOR EARLIER.>
<YOU SEE, I'VE LIVED IN THE STATES UP UNTIL LAST MONTH.>
<I LEARNED ABOUT JAPAN AND STUDIED JAPANESE, BUT I DON'T UNDERSTAND EVERYTHING YET...>
<WELL...>

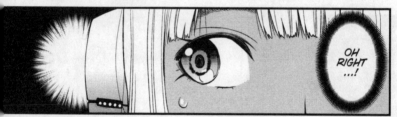

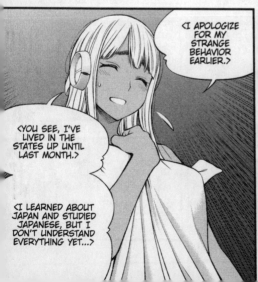

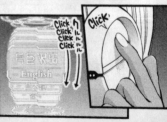

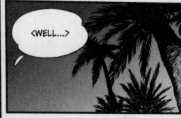

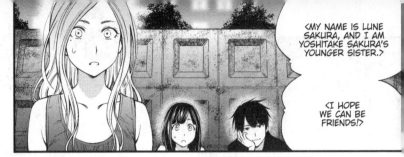

<MY NAME IS LUNE SAKURA, AND I AM YOSHITAKE SAKURA'S YOUNGER SISTER.>

<I HOPE WE CAN BE FRIENDS!>

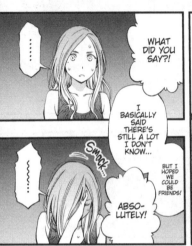

......

WHAT DID YOU SAY?!

I BASICALLY SAID THERE'S STILL A LOT I DON'T KNOW...

BUT I HOPED WE COULD BE FRIENDS!

ABSO-LUTELY!

......

Smooch...

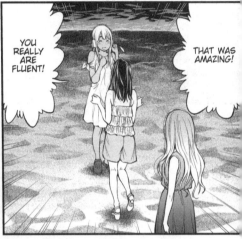

YOU REALLY ARE FLUENT!

THAT WAS AMAZING!

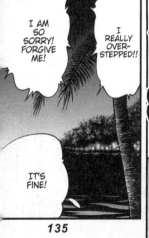

I AM SO SORRY! FORGIVE ME!

I REALLY OVER-STEPPED!!

IT'S FINE!

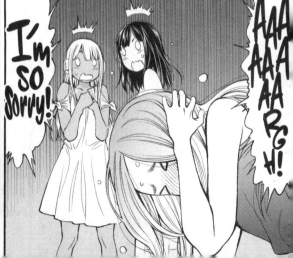

I'M SO SORRY!

AAAAAAAARGH!

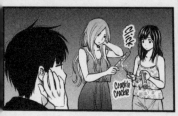

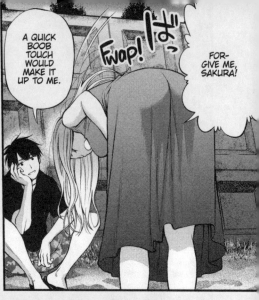

A QUICK BOOB TOUCH WOULD MAKE IT UP TO ME.

FORGIVE ME, SAKURA!

Fwap!

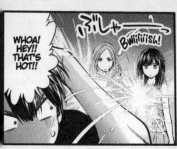

WHOA! HEY!! THAT'S HOT!!

Bwiiiiish!

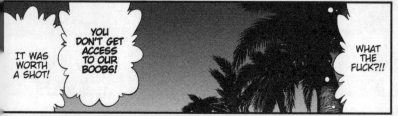

IT WAS WORTH A SHOT!

YOU DON'T GET ACCESS TO OUR BOOBS!

WHAT THE FUCK?!!

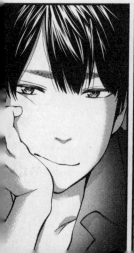

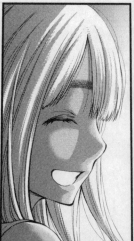

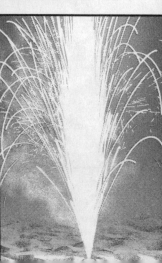

カポーン
ka-pooon
Hngah!

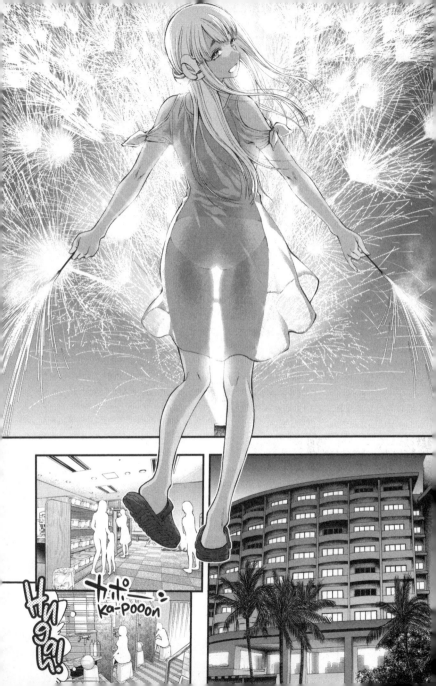

IT HURTS...
WHY DOES MY SKIN STING LIKE THIS...?
Tingle
Tingle
Sting
Sting
Sting
YOU'RE SUN-BURNED!
YOU DIDN'T TAN AT ALL, MIKA-SAN.
I NEVER BURN!
BOY, I SURE DO.
I SEE...
SO THIS IS A SUN-BURN!!
THE SUN...
IS AMAZING ...!
......
THEN AGAIN...

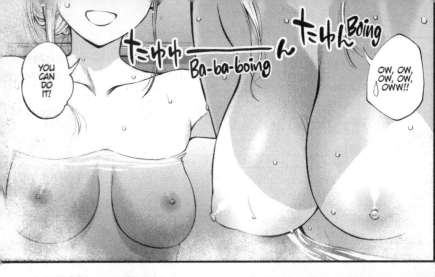

たゆ——ん Ba-ba-boing ん たゆん Boing

YOU CAN DO IT!

OW, OW, OW, OW, OWW!!

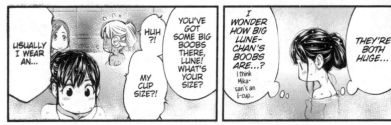

USUALLY I WEAR AN...

HUH ?!

MY CUP SIZE?!

YOU'VE GOT SOME BIG BOOBS THERE, LUNE! WHAT'S YOUR SIZE?

I WONDER HOW BIG LUNE-CHAN'S BOOBS ARE...? I think Mika-san's an E-cup...

THEY'RE BOTH HUGE...

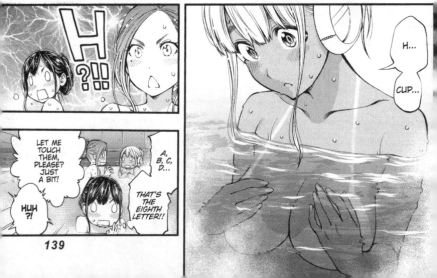

H ?!!

H... CUP...

LET ME TOUCH THEM, PLEASE? JUST A BIT!

HUH ?!

A, B, C, D...

THAT'S THE EIGHTH LETTER!!

139

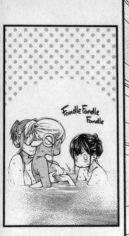

Fondle Fondle
Fondle

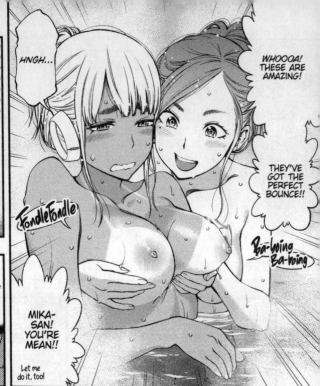

HNGH...

WHOOOA! THESE ARE AMAZING!

THEY'VE GOT THE PERFECT BOUNCE!!

Ba-boing Ba-boing

Fondle Fondle

MIKA-SAN! YOU'RE MEAN!!

Let me do it, too!

THESE...

ARE AMAZ-ING!!!

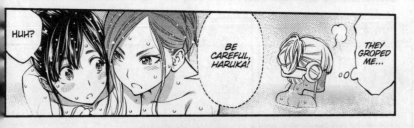

HUH?

BE CAREFUL, HARUKA!

THEY GROPED ME...

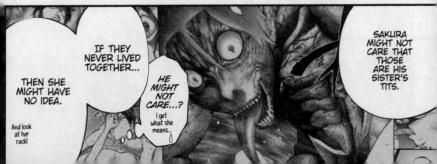

IF THEY NEVER LIVED TOGETHER...

THEN SHE MIGHT HAVE NO IDEA.

And look at her rack!

HE MIGHT NOT CARE...?

I get what she means...

SAKURA MIGHT NOT CARE THAT THOSE ARE HIS SISTER'S TITS.

THERE'S NO TELLING WHEN AN ACCIDENT COULD HAPPEN ...!!!
ど————ん
Ba-boom
ACCI-DENT!!
NOOOOOOOOOOO
I DON'T WANT THAT!!

142

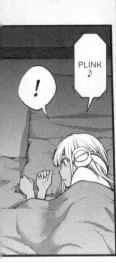

! PLINK ♪

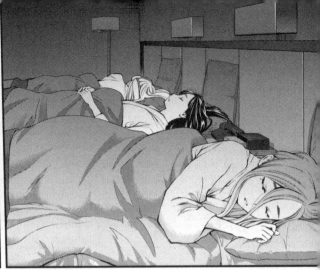

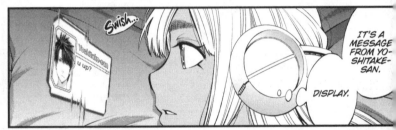

Swish...

IT'S A MESSAGE FROM YO-SHITAKE-SAN.

Yoshitake-san
u up?

DISPLAY.

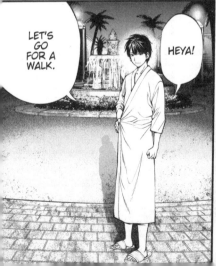

LET'S GO FOR A WALK.

HEYA!

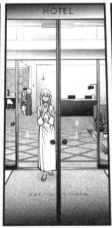

HOTEL

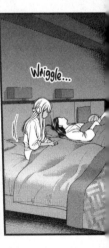

Wriggle...

THE NIGHT BREEZE FEELS GREAT!
Really?
IT'S LUKEWARM AND HUMID.
Fwa-zssshh...
ザザァ...
SOMETHING ABOUT THE OCEAN BEING PITCH BLACK AT NIGHT IS KINDA SCARY...
IT WAS PRETTY DURING THE DAY.
IT'S JUST LIKE HOW PEOPLE ARE. THEY SMILE CHEERFULLY IN YOUR FACE...
AND THEY HAVE A DARK SIDE TO THEM, AS WELL.

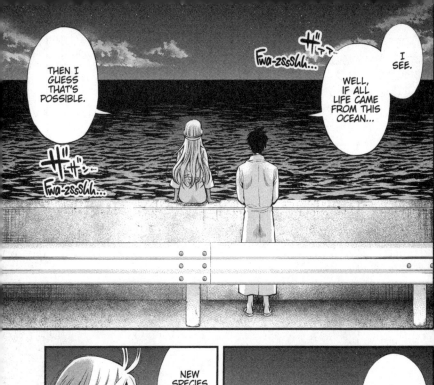

THEN I GUESS THAT'S POSSIBLE.

I SEE.

WELL, IF ALL LIFE CAME FROM THIS OCEAN...

Fwa-zssshh...

Fwa-zssshh...

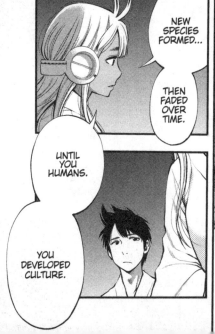

NEW SPECIES FORMED...

THEN FADED OVER TIME.

UNTIL YOU HUMANS.

YOU DEVELOPED CULTURE.

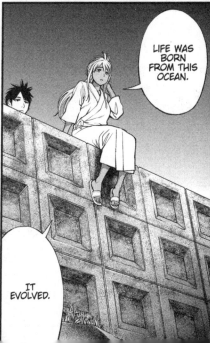

LIFE WAS BORN FROM THIS OCEAN.

IT EVOLVED.

YOU LEARNED TO COOPERATE.
MALES WERE NO LONGER WARRIORS AND LOVERS.
PEACETIME MADE THEM LESS VIGOROUS.
ULTIMATELY...
THEY BECAME FEMINIZED!
NOT THAT FEMALES LACKED SEX DRIVE.
THEY WERE JUST AS... WELL...
IS SHE TALKING ABOUT SUPOPOPON...?
OR COULD IT BE...
BUT FEMALES LIKE TAME MALES.
SO LOW-TESTOSTERONE MALES WON, IN THE END.
CONFLICT IS NON-EXISTENT ON SUPOPOPON.
IT'S A PEACEFUL PLANET...
BUT WE HAVE LOST THE INSTINCT TO REPRODUCE.

ARE WE...
DESTINED TO GO EXTINCT?
NN...
Jolt!

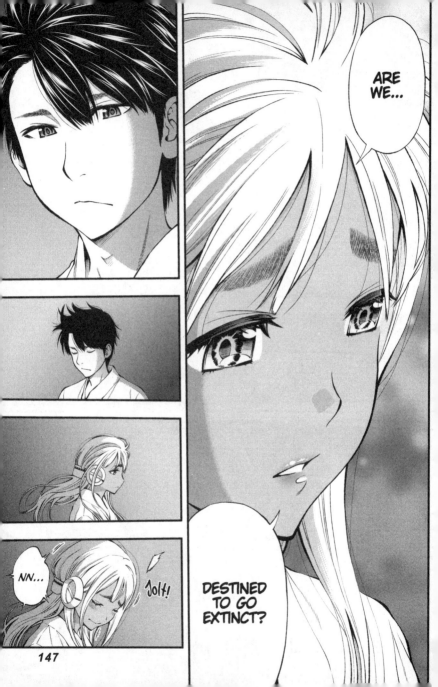

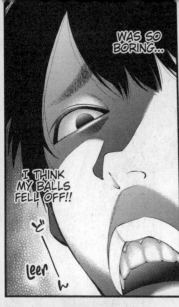

WAS SO BORING...

I THINK MY BALLS FELL OFF!!

Leer

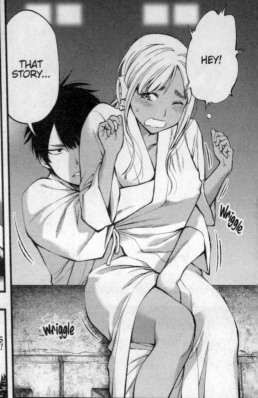

THAT STORY...

HEY!

Wriggle

Wriggle

BUT...

THAT'S MEAN!!

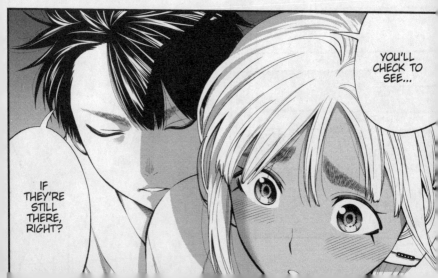

YOU'LL CHECK TO SEE...

IF THEY'RE STILL THERE, RIGHT?

I'LL SAVE YOUR PLANET.
NN...
SMOOCH
NO...
NOT...
HERE...
Mn...

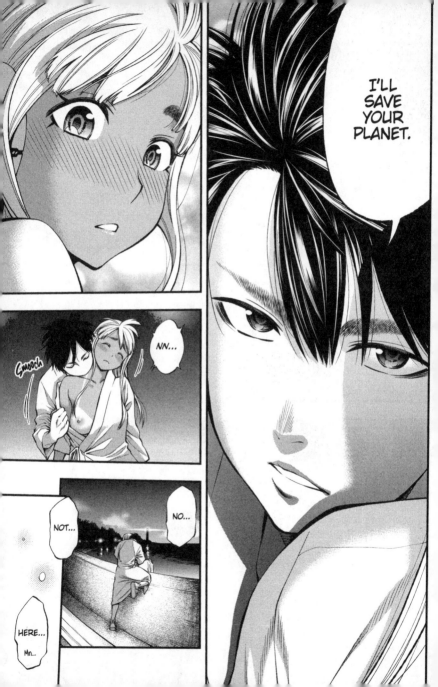

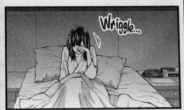

Wriggle...

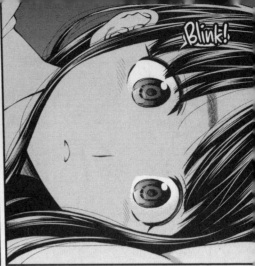

Blink!

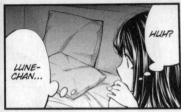

HUH?

LUNE-CHAN...

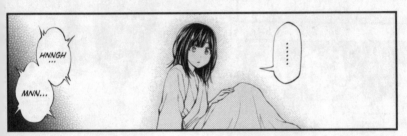

HNNGH...

MNN...

......

......

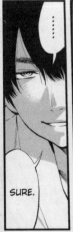

......

SURE.

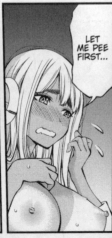

LET ME PEE FIRST...

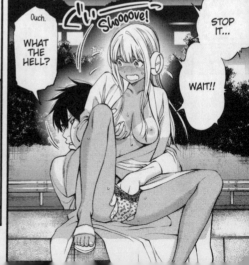

Ouch.

WHAT THE HELL?

Shoooove!

STOP IT...

WAIT!!

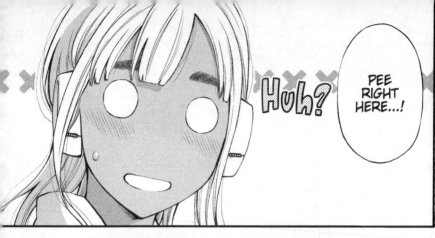

Huh?

PEE RIGHT HERE...!

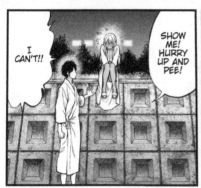

I CAN'T!!

SHOW ME! HURRY UP AND PEE!

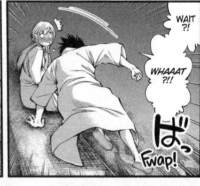

WAIT ?!

WHAAAT ?!!

Fwap!

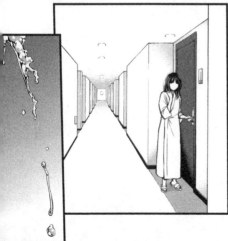

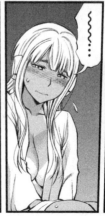

......!

COME ON!

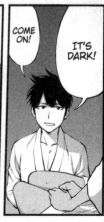

IT'S DARK!

Plip

Plip...　Plip

Paaant
Pant...
Pant...
ぽた Plip
Plip ぽた
AH...
Pant...
PEE-PEE...
Pant...
HNNNNGAH!!
Shudder
No...
NOT THERE ...
Shlip...
IT'S DIRTY...
Shlip...
Mmf! ....!
Jolt!
Quiver!
Huff...

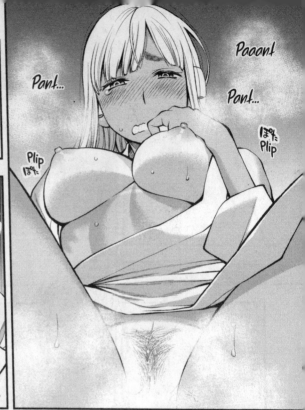

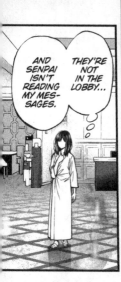

AND SENPAI ISN'T READING MY MESSAGES.

THEY'RE NOT IN THE LOBBY...

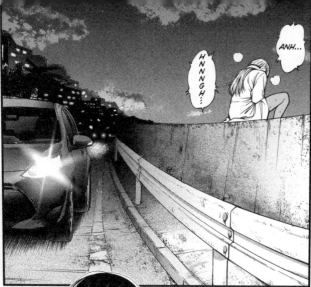

ANH...

HNNNGH...

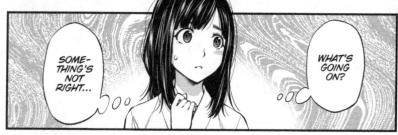

SOMETHING'S NOT RIGHT...

WHAT'S GOING ON?

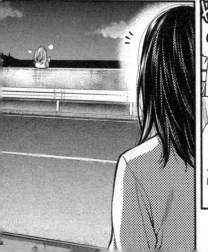

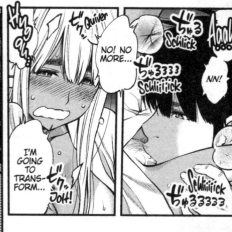

Fya

Quiver

Schlick

Aggh

NO! NO MORE...

Schliiiick

NN!

I'M GOING TO TRANSFORM...

Jolt!

Schliiiick

Quiver!
Eeep
Jolt!!
LUNE-CHAN!!
!!
Bump!!
?!!

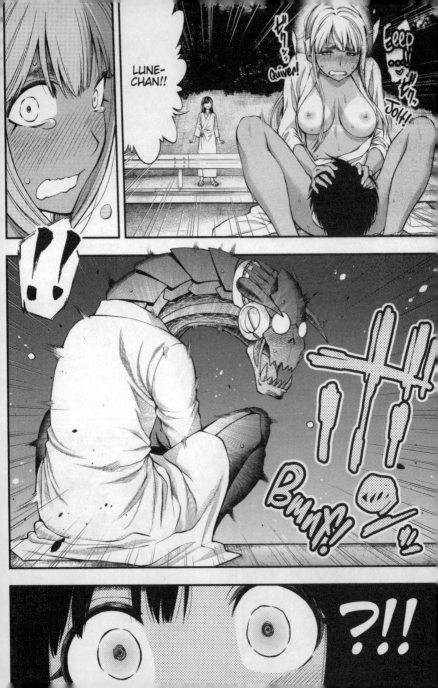

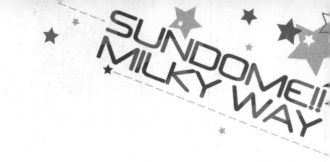

SUNDOME!!
MILKY WAY

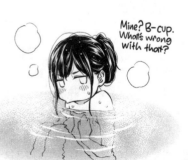

Mine? B-cup.
What's wrong
with that?

Stopping Point!!
Young Jump Edition
DON'T TOUCH
DON'T TOUCH
DON'T TOUCH
DON'T TOUCH
DON'T TOUCH
DON'T TOUCH

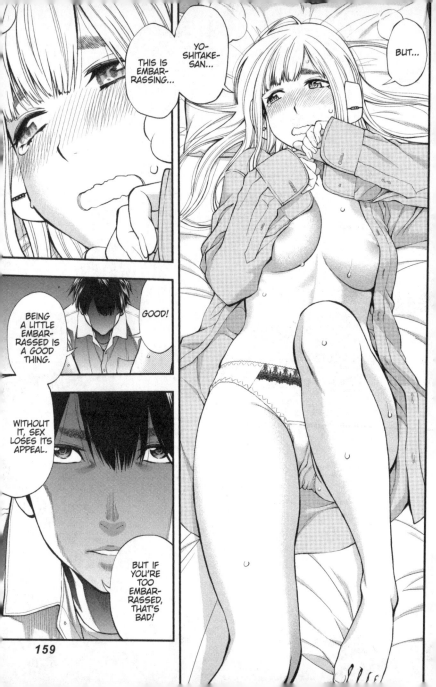

THIS IS EMBARRASSING...

YO-SHITAKE-SAN...

BUT...

BEING A LITTLE EMBARRASSED IS A GOOD THING.

GOOD!

WITHOUT IT, SEX LOSES ITS APPEAL.

BUT IF YOU'RE TOO EMBARRASSED, THAT'S BAD!

GRAPPLE
THAT'S WHY!!
EEEEEK!
わしっ
YOU MUST PERSE-VERE!!
OVERCOME THESE FEELINGS!
ぶるぶる Bounce Bounce
ぽよぽよ
ぶるぽよ saish saish
Bounce Bounce ぶるぽよ
saish saish
HEY...!
ぶるるん Ba-boing
MNNF ...!
ぽよよん Jiggle
Bounce Bounce
ぶるぶる saish saish
ぽよぽよ
ぶるぽよ saish saish
Bounce Bounce ぶるぽよ
CONQUER YOUR SHAME!!
すぺたん すぺたん
Sh-pa-plap Sh-pa-plap
WELL?! IS THIS EMBAR-RASSING?!
DON'T PLAY WITH THEM...!
たぷ Ba-boing
たぷ Ba-boing
Nn!
STOP...
すぺたん すぺたん
Sh-pa-plap Sh-pa-plap
HNNGH!
SmackSmack
ぴしぴし
ぴしぴし
SmackSmack
BUT CONQUER IT!
NN...
FEEL SHAME!
NO... ANH!!
Shma-smack
Shma-smack
Smack-ack-ack-ack-ack-ack

BURN WITH IT!
ベロベロベロ
ベロベロベロ
ベロベロベロ
Slurp
Slurp
Slurp
Slurp Slurp Slurp
Slurp Slurp Slurp
Slurp Slurp
Quiver ビクッ
Quiver ビクッ
FEEL THE SHAME!!!
AAAANGH...
ANH?!
AH!
Slurp Slurp Slurp
ベロベロベロ Slurp
ベロベロベロ Slurp
Slurp ベロベロベロ
Slurp Slurp Slurp Slurp Slurp
TOO PHILOSOPHICAL...
Aaanh!
Scquel-el-el-el-el-echhhhhh!!!
Angh...
Ah!
じゅぼぼぼぼぼぼ
Schquelee-e-e-ch!
ビクッ Jolt
Aaanh!
Hugaaaaaaaaaah!!
Slurp Slurp Slurp
ベロベロベロ Slurp
ベロベロベロ Slurp
ベロベロベロ Slurp
Slurp Slurp Slurp
Squuu-i-i-ich!
ゴシゴシゴシゴシ
RUB RUB RUB RUB
RUB RUB RUB RUB RUB RUB RUB
ゴシゴシゴシゴシ
ゴシゴシゴシゴシ
ゴシゴシゴシゴシ
RUB RUB RUB RUB RUB RUB RUB RUB
Jolt
Jeez...!
No...!
ビクッ JOLT!
Stop it!!
ビクッ Quiver!
ビクッ
JOLT!
Squilch! Squilch! Squuiilch!
Quiver!

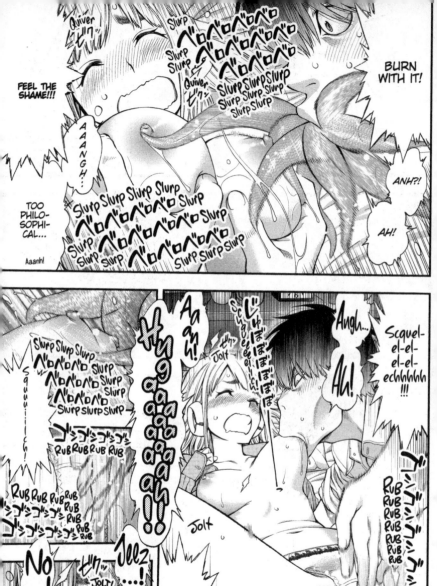

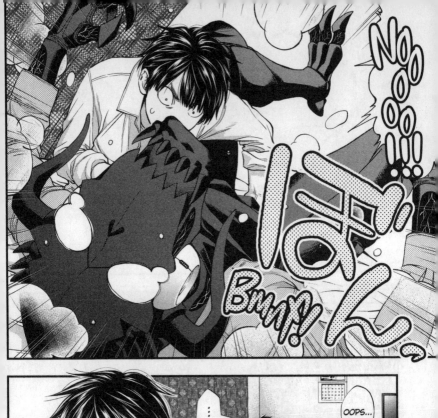

NOOOOO!!!

BMMF!!

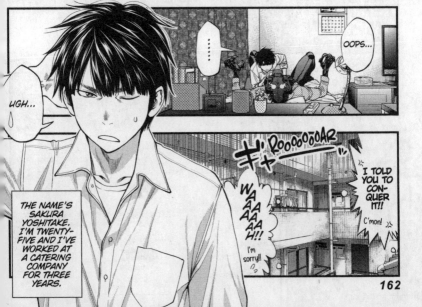

......

OOPS...

UGH...

ROOOOOOAR

I TOLD YOU TO CONQUER IT!!

C'MON!

WAAAAAH!!

I'm sorry!!

THE NAME'S SAKURA YOSHITAKE. I'M TWENTY-FIVE AND I'VE WORKED AT A CATERING COMPANY FOR THREE YEARS.

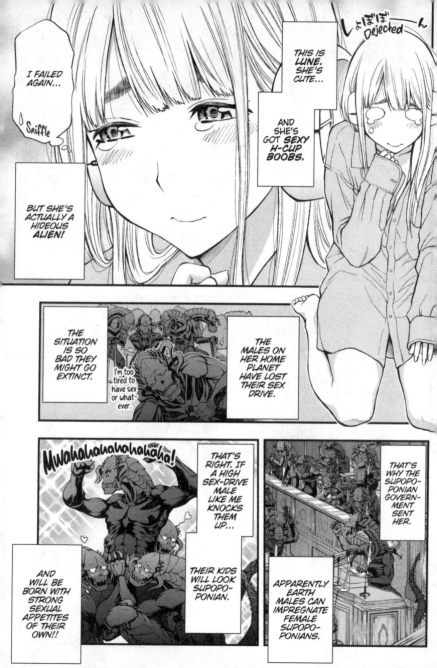

しょぼぼ―――ん
Dejected

THIS IS LUNE. SHE'S CUTE...

AND SHE'S GOT *SEXY H-CUP BOOBS.*

I FAILED AGAIN...

Sniffle

BUT SHE'S ACTUALLY A *HIDEOUS ALIEN!*

THE SITUATION IS SO BAD THEY MIGHT GO EXTINCT.

I'm too tired to have sex or whatever.

THE MALES ON HER HOME PLANET HAVE LOST THEIR SEX DRIVE.

Mwahahahahahahahaha!

THAT'S RIGHT. IF A HIGH SEX-DRIVE MALE LIKE ME KNOCKS THEM UP...

THEIR KIDS WILL LOOK SUPOPO-PONIAN.

THAT'S WHY THE SUPOPO-PONIAN GOVERN-MENT SENT HER.

AND WILL BE BORN WITH STRONG SEXUAL APPETITES OF THEIR OWN!!

APPARENTLY EARTH MALES CAN IMPREGNATE FEMALE SUPOPO-PONIANS.

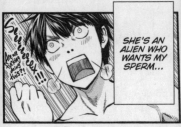

SHE'S AN ALIEN WHO WANTS MY SPERM...

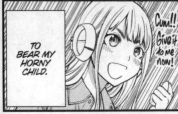

TO BEAR MY HORNY CHILD.

Cum!! Give it to me now!

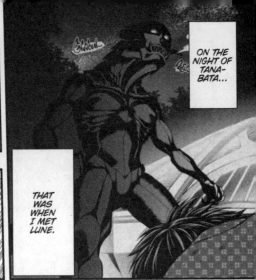

ON THE NIGHT OF TANA-BATA...

THAT WAS WHEN I MET LUNE.

BUT...

YOU'D THINK IT'D BE EASIER TO JIZZ HER...

HER CUNT'S THE WRONG SHAPE.

NOT ONLY IS SHE HIDEOUS...

WE'VE BEEN TRYING TO TRAIN LUNE TO FUCK.

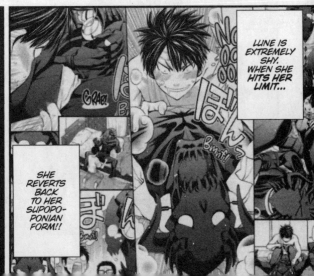

LUNE IS EXTREMELY SHY. WHEN SHE HITS HER LIMIT...

SHE REVERTS BACK TO HER SUPOPO-PONIAN FORM!!

DOES IT FIT?
YUP!
DRESS LIKE A SLUT, BE A SLUT!
IT SEEMS LIKE... I'm missing a lot of clothing here...
MY BOOBS ARE EX-POSED...
AND...
DROP THEM PANTIES. NOW!
Eh heh heh...
Huh ...?

たゆゆーん
Boing-ba-boing
ぷりりーん
Soft & Plump
I CAN FEEL A DRAFT ON MY BUTT...
SO WHAT ARE YOU DOING, EXACTLY?
I THOUGHT I'D MAKE DINNER.
DINNER ...?
Can you even cook?
THE POTATOES SHE CUT ARE...
The skin's still on them...
Blub-ub-ub-ub-ub
See!!
DON'T TELL ME YOU THINK THAT'S ALL IT TAKES?

THAT'S NOT REALLY COOKING, EITHER...

THEN AT LEAST LET ME COOK EGG ON RICE!

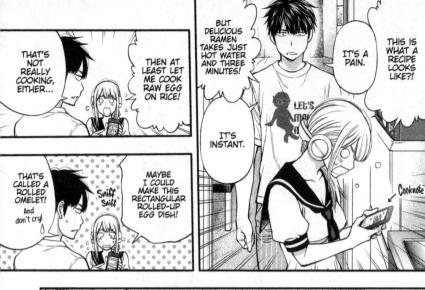

BUT DELICIOUS RAMEN TAKES JUST HOT WATER AND THREE MINUTES!

IT'S INSTANT.

IT'S A PAIN.

THIS IS WHAT A RECIPE LOOKS LIKE?!

THAT'S CALLED A ROLLED OMELET!

And don't cry!

Sniff Sniff

MAYBE I COULD MAKE THIS RECTANGULAR ROLLED-UP EGG DISH!

Cooknote

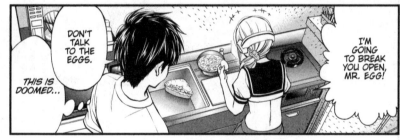

DON'T TALK TO THE EGGS.

THIS IS DOOMED...

I'M GOING TO BREAK YOU OPEN, MR. EGG!

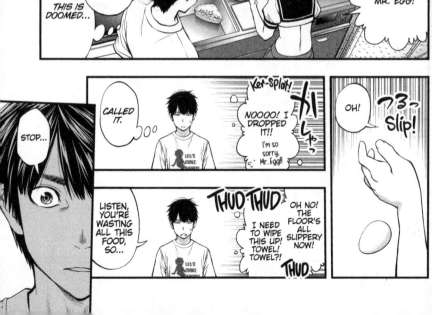

STOP...

CALLED IT.

Ker-splat!

NOOOOO! I DROPPED IT!!

I'm so sorry, Mr. Egg!!

OH!

Slip!

LISTEN, YOU'RE WASTING ALL THIS FOOD, SO...

THUD THUD

I NEED TO WIPE THIS UP! TOWEL! TOWEL?!

OH NO! THE FLOOR'S ALL SLIPPERY NOW!

THUD

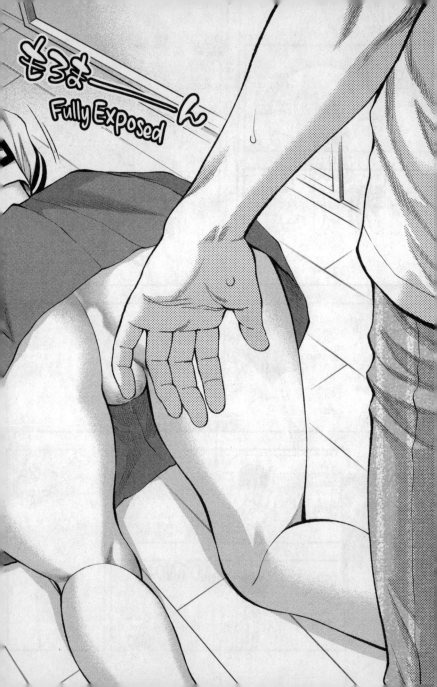

もろまーん
Fully Exposed

ゴシ
Rub Ru
ゴシ
Rub
HUFF...
UNF...
GRAB!
がばあっ
FUCK YESSS!!!
!!
Hngaaaaaaaaaaaah!!!
Bmuf!
NO, WAIT...! JUST A BIT MORE...
UGGGH...

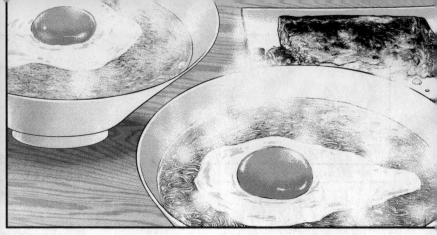

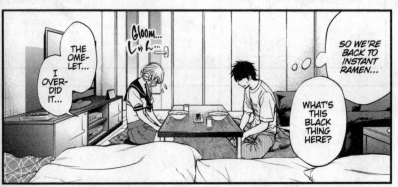

THE OMELET... I OVERDID IT...

Gloom... じゅん...

SO WE'RE BACK TO INSTANT RAMEN...

WHAT'S THIS BLACK THING HERE?

I'LL SHOW YOU ANOTHER TIME...

AND WHEN WILL THAT BE?!

ACTUALLY...

I'VE CERTAINLY NEVER SEEN THESE TECHNIQUES!

IT WAS ALL SEXY SIMULATIONS AND TECHNIQUES...

NO, NOT REALLY...

Blllsh!

YOU SAID YOU WERE TRAINED FOR THIS MISSION.

YES! I WAS!

THEY DIDN'T TEACH YOU TO COOK?

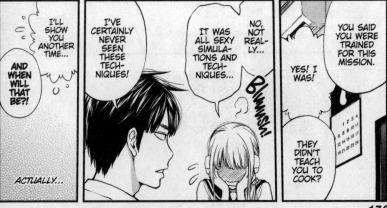

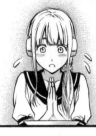

JUST TO CLAIM MY SPERM...

SHE CAME ALL THE WAY TO ANOTHER PLANET...

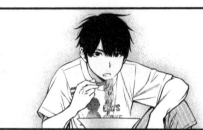

BUT IS THAT WHAT SHE WANTS?

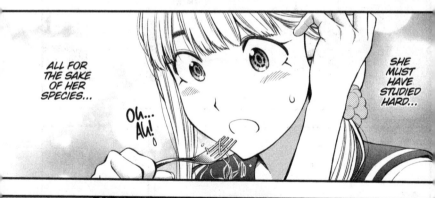

ALL FOR THE SAKE OF HER SPECIES...

Oh... Ah!

SHE MUST HAVE STUDIED HARD...

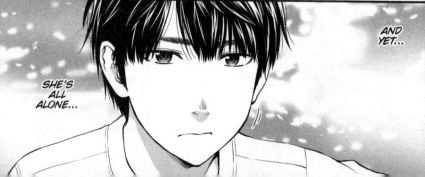

AND YET...

SHE'S ALL ALONE...

WELP.
HUFF...
NOT LIKE I GIVE A FUCK!
MNN...
IF WE DO IT...

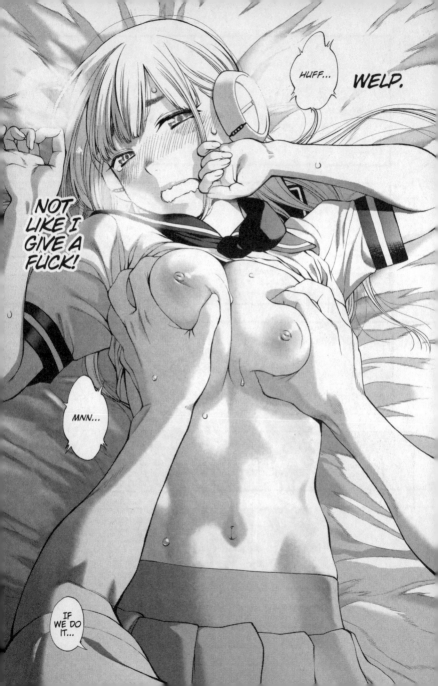

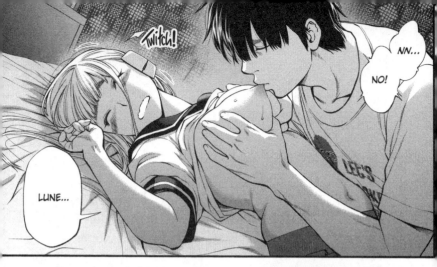

NN...

NO!

LUNE...

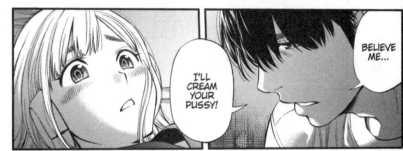

BELIEVE ME...

I'LL CREAM YOUR PUSSY!

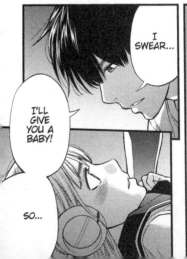

I SWEAR...

I'LL GIVE YOU A BABY!

SO...

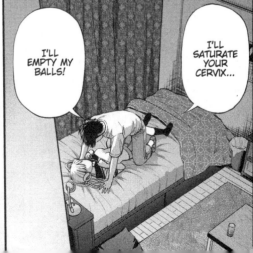

I'LL EMPTY MY BALLS!

I'LL SATURATE YOUR CERVIX...

GIVE IN TO ME!
OKAY...

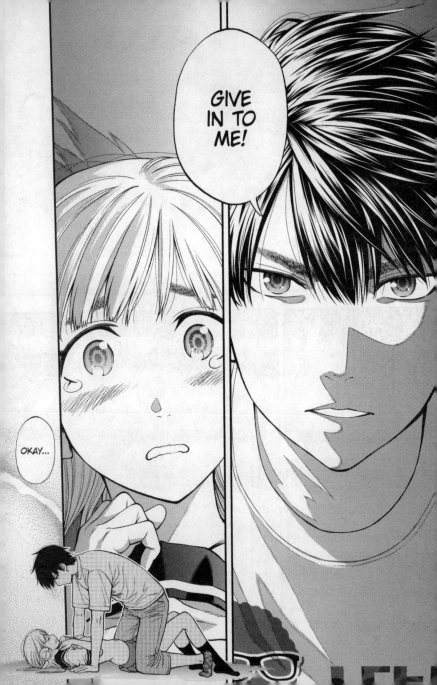

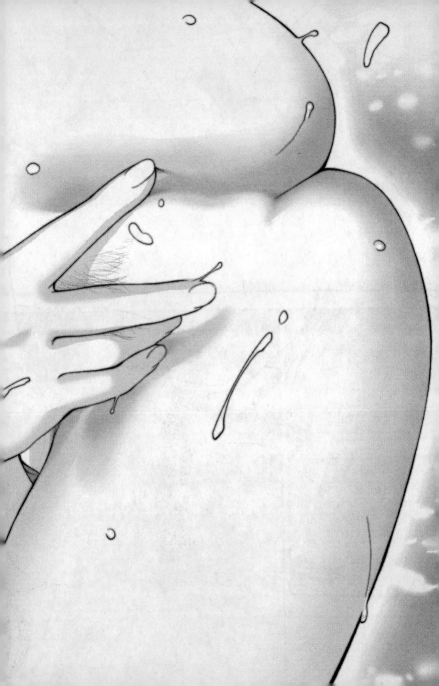

SO...

WHAT THE FUCK...
ち—ん
Ding...
I'M SO SORRY...

WHY ARE YOU LIKE THIS?!
THAT WAS QUICKER THAN USUAL!
Your heart's not in this!
IT IS, IT IS!
うわーーん
Waaaaaaaaaah!
YOU MIGHT AS WELL GO HOME!
THAT WAS MEAN!!
VILLAGE KING

LUNE CHAN...
Bmuf!
Has Lune's true form been discovered?!!
What will Lune do now?!!
Is she about to be sent home for goo
What's going to happen?!!
I'LL LET YOU LOCK YOURSELF AWAY!
WHY THE HELL DO I HAVE TO HIDE HERE?!
I'M THE ONLY ONE WHO NEEDS TO HIDE, RIGHT?!
BOOBS.
Why is Yoshitake locked up with Mika-san in a locker?!!
Volume 3
SUNDOME!! MILKY WAY
Going on Sale
February 2022

SEVEN SEAS' GHOST SHIP PRESENTS

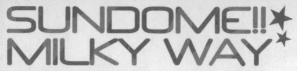

SUNDOME!!★ MILKY WAY★

story and art by KAZUKI FUNATSU — VOLUME 2

TRANSLATION
Joshua Hardy

ADAPTATION
The Smut Whisperer

LETTERING
Joven Voon

COVER DESIGN
Nicky Lim

LOGO DESIGN
George Panella

PROOFREADER
Janet Houck

COPY EDITOR
Dawn Davis

EDITOR
Nick Mamatas

PREPRESS TECHNICIAN
Rhiannon Rasmussen-Silverstein

PRODUCTION MANAGER - GHOST SHIP
George Panella

PRODUCTION MANAGER
Lissa Pattillo

MANAGING EDITOR
Julie Davis

ASSOCIATE PUBLISHER
Adam Arnold

PUBLISHER
Jason DeAngelis

Seven Seas press and purchase enquiries can be sent to Marketing Manager Lianne Sentar at press@gomanga.com. Information regarding the distribution and purchase of digital editions is available from Digital Manager CK Russell at digital@gomanga.com.

Seven Seas and the Seven Seas logo are trademarks of Seven Seas Entertainment. All rights reserved.

ISBN: 978-1-64827-624-8
Printed in Canada
First Printing: November 2021
10 9 8 7 6 5 4 3 2 1

///// READING DIRECTIONS /////

This book reads from *right to left*, Japanese style. If this is your first time reading manga, you start reading from the top right panel on each page and take it from there. If you get lost, just follow the numbered diagram here. It may seem backwards at first, but you'll get the hang of it! Have fun!!

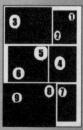

Follow us online: www.GhostShipManga.com